The Leadership Framework Series

THE WAY TO GO

HOW TO
Maximize Workplace Capability

T0363140

PETER MILLS

The Way to Go: How to Maximize Workplace Capability
Peter Mills © 2019

National Library of Australia Cataloguing-in-Publication entry:

Creator:	Mills, Peter, author
Title:	The Way to Go: How to Maximize Workplace Capability
ISBN:	9781925962031 (paperback)
Series:	Leadership Framework Series
Subjects:	Business planning
	Strategic planning.
	Executive ability.
	Management.
	Organizational effectiveness.
	Success in business.
	Human Resources.
	Training and Development

Published by Peter Mills, InHouse Publishing, and GOKO Publishing

Acknowledgments

I WISH TO THANK Barry and Sheila Deane, from PeopleFit Australasia, who developed the original Leadership Framework based on the work of Elliott Jaques and Lord Wilfred Brown. They have kindly given me full access to their substantial and excellent work, without which I could not have written this book. I also wish to acknowledge Therese Harris and Amy Mizalski, two HR professionals, whom I have worked with for a number of years, both of whom reviewed drafts of this book and made valuable suggestions for improvement.

Finally, I would also like to thank my wife, Sue, who reviewed the book and helped me to clarify my thoughts and ideas.

Using This Book

THIS BOOK IS ONE OF FOUR BOOKS based on The Leadership Framework, a holistic and integrated framework for organizational and managerial leadership. As all books in the series are based on the same framework, the concepts are aligned, and they use consistent terms, definitions, principles, concepts and methods. Together, these books provide leaders with an integrated methodology for all aspects of people management and together they are a powerful tool for leaders at all levels.

This book provides leaders and human resources professionals with the information and resources they need to improve workforce capability. The book provides:

- A model for workforce capability development.
- An understanding of individual capability.
- An understanding of what aspects of individual capability can and cannot be developed.
- The impacts of the working organization on individual and organizational capability.
- Specific examples of actions that can be undertaken to improve both individual and workforce capability.

While no book could provide detailed information on every aspect of workforce capability, the focus here is to provide a good starting point.

Each chapter has a clear summary of the key points and some tips for getting started. There is also a companion website available for those who want to access additional information and tools:

www.theleadershipframework.com.au

Contents

Chapter 1

What is workforce capability?

Workforce capability is an organization's ability to accomplish its objectives through its people. This not only requires people with the right individual capability, it also requires the working organization to operate effectively.

WORKING ORGANIZATIONS ARE MADE UP of people, and it is people who create and deliver an organization's products and services. People also manage the organization's infrastructure, including its physical, financial and people assets. Therefore, having an organization full of capable and committed people is essential to achieve business goals. However, even if the best people are employed, it is still not enough to ensure that an organization will operate to its full potential, as the work environment itself must support productive work and enable all employees to work together effectively.

Therefore, workforce capability is more than just having capable employees. It also requires an effective working organization that both enables and sustains productive work. Both components are necessary (i.e. capable people and an effective working organization).

What are capable people?

Capable people are those with the individual capability to perform the work of their role to the required standard. This is more than a person's knowledge, skills and experience. While these are essential, they are only one component of individual capability. The Leadership Framework defines individual capability as a person's:

> unique combination of knowledge, skills and experience and their level of work ability to solve the complexity of problems in a role. To perform successfully also requires them to value the work sufficiently to release energy and commitment to sustain high performance, plus an absence of personal, disabling temperament.

This multi-dimensional definition is represented in the diagram below.

The individual's capability profile

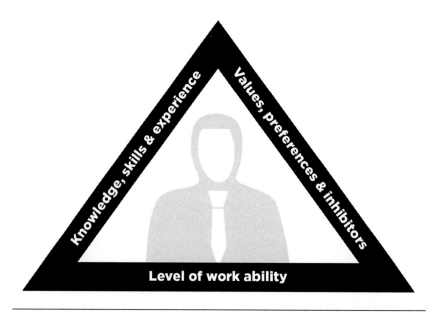

In this definition, it is the accumulation of all aspects of a person's capability that enables that person to perform effectively. In analyzing each component of individual capability, we find:

i.   Knowledge, skills and experience (KSE).

In order to work effectively, a person must have a certain knowledge, background, training and education. *Knowledge* is what they have learned. They must also know how to apply their knowledge. *Skill* is the ability to apply their knowledge. Using knowledge and skills provides people with the *experience* so they can learn what works best in each situation. Examples of knowledge, skills and experience include:

- The ability to understand the financial impact of plans, decisions and actions.
- The ability to work effectively in large project teams.
- The ability to build effective teams, set direction and get commitment from team members.

Where a person's knowledge and skills and experience are less than the role's requirements, managerial coaching and training can be effective in improving individual capability.

ii.   Values, preferences and inhibitors (VP&I).

To perform at a high standard continuously, a person must value their work. *Values* and *preferences* determine the types of work that individuals do well, that is, what they are intrinsically motivated to do. Valuing the work is about the person's level of interest, commitment to and sense of achievement in what they do.

Where an individual does not find value, or is not interested, or finds no enjoyment in a particular kind of work (e.g. managing people, analysis or detailed work) they are unlikely to be able to sustain effort over time or to excel in their role, even though they have the knowledge, skills and experience to do the work. In cases where an individual does not value the work at all, they may not even be able to sustain an effort to meet minimum performance requirements. A symptom of not valuing the work may be a reluctance to accept accountability for their work or poor behaviors such as timekeeping, non-delivery or a lack of interest in the work.

While valuing the work is not about individual values per se, valuing the work does extend to organizational fit, where an individual's compatibility with an organization's products or mode of operation does not match the organization. For example, a non-smoker may not want to work for a tobacco company as they do not believe in their product.

If a person does not value their work, although they have all the inherent requirements of the role, they are unlikely to consistently perform at a high level. Training will not assist. The action required is to transfer the person to a suitable role or to initiate removal.

Individual capability is also inhibited by poor behavior. *Inhibitors* are extremes of behavior, which get in the way of working. Inhibitors refer to the ability of each person to act in line with the behaviors valued or expressed in their organization. They are not job-specific. These may include: chronic problems with interpersonal relationships, aggression, disabling extremes of temperament, drug or alcohol dependency.

Where an individual's capability to perform a role is overshadowed by one or more negative personal characteristics, a manager must ensure the person is aware of their behavior by offering clear and unambiguous feedback on the impact on their work performance and assert the requirements and the consequences. Training will not assist. It is for the individual to decide if they want to change. If they cannot or will not change, then the manager must initiate removal.

iii. Level of work ability (LoWA).

The third part of individual capability is a person's level of work ability. *Level of work ability* is an individual's cognitive ability to assimilate data and information and to exercise sound judgment in the face of ambiguity and uncertainty. Level of work ability enables people to deal with particular levels of complexity of information – different classes of problems, where facts are not available and solutions are not obvious.

According to Elliott Jaques, level of work ability differs naturally in individuals and is distributed in all populations in the same manner. It is innate and unfolds throughout life. The maturation process of each person's complexity of information processing cannot be speeded up or enhanced by special education or occupational opportunities, or impeded by less favorable social, educational or occupational opportunities. It is natural, unfolding and predictable.

The extent to which the individual's LoWA is higher or lower than the requirements of the role will have predictable consequences.

- If a person's LoWA is higher than the role, they will feel under-utilized or get distracted by trying to find work at a higher level to satisfy them. They may try to grow their role and tasks so they are more satisfied.
- If a person's LoWA is lower than that required for the role, they will not be able to solve the problems of the role and cannot therefore meet the role requirements. They will shrink their role and tasks to the level of work in which they can operate most comfortably.

In either case, training will not assist. The person must be moved to a suitable role or the manager must initial removal.

So, why is this model for individual capability important for workforce capability?

When a person's individual capability matches the work, not only will they do a good job, the person will also feel a sense of satisfaction and well-being in carrying out their work. Understanding individual capability enables managers and whole organizations to take the appropriate corrective action to improve individual capability, as not all issues around individual capability require training. Often other managerial action is required.

What is an effective working organization?

The second component of workforce capability is an effective working organization. Having a capable workforce requires having capable people in the right roles, all working to their full potential. Two of the founding principles in The Leadership Framework are:

- *The work environment critically influences the individual's ability to do their best work.*
- *Productive work is enabled by systemic trust and fairness and is reduced by fear.*

Therefore, to enable people to work to their full potential, each component of the working organization must be designed and built to operate effectively. Failure to deliver the basic infrastructure of the working organization will directly impact the personal effectiveness of all employees.

So, what is the *working organization*?

An effective working organization consists of:

- A clear purpose and direction.
- A purpose-built organizational structure (i.e. functions, roles and role relationships).
- Integrated and fit for purpose systems of work (policies, processes and information and communication technologies).
- Consistent and effective managerial leadership practices.

Each component creates the working environment in which people work.

The working organization

Without clear direction, an effective structure (with clearly defined roles and role relationships) and integrated systems of work – all activated by effective managerial leadership practices - the organization's strategy and purpose may not be able to be delivered. The causes of failure will not be clear. Focus will be on the capability of the individual and not the working organization.

Therefore, as workforce capability has two components, individual capability and an effective working organization, to improve workforce capability requires improvement in the capability of every individual employee and in the management of the impacts of the working organization on employee effectiveness.

Key Concepts

- Workforce capability is more than just having capable employees. It also requires an effective working organization that both enables and sustains productive work. Failure to deliver the basic infrastructure of the working organization will directly impact the personal effectiveness of all employees.

- Capable people are those with the individual capability to perform the work of their role to the required standard. The Leadership Framework defines individual capability as a person's:

  unique combination of knowledge, skills and experience and their level of work ability to solve the complexity of problems in a role. To perform successfully also requires them to value the work sufficiently to release energy and commitment to sustain high performance, plus an absence of personal, disabling temperament.

- An effective working organization consists of:
  - A clear purpose and direction.
  - A purpose-built organizational structure (i.e. functions, roles and role relationships).
  - Integrated and fit for purpose systems of work (policies, processes and information and communication technologies).
  - Consistent and effective managerial leadership practices.

- As workforce capability has two components, individual capability and an effective working organization, to improve workforce capability requires improvement in the capability of every individual employee and in the management of the impacts of the working organization on employee effectiveness.

Tips for Getting Started

1. Assess how your organization defines individual capability. Does this need to be adjusted to take into account components in The Leadership Framework's model for individual capability?
2. When considering employee effectiveness, how are the impacts of the working organization on employee performance assessed?
3. To gain a better understanding of the concepts of the impact of the working organization on each employee's personal effectiveness, read the second book in the Leadership Framework Series titled, *Don't Fix Me, Fix the Workplace: A Guide to Building Constructive Working Relationships* by Peter Mills.

Additional information available at www.theleadershipframework.com.au

- Introduction to The Leadership Framework.
- Creating a workforce capability strategy – overview.

Chapter 2

What is a workforce capability strategy?

A good workforce capability strategy clearly defines the workforce requirements to deliver the organization's objectives together with the prioritized actions required to achieve these requirements.

A WORKFORCE CAPABILITY STRATEGY is one component of an organization's strategic planning process. A workforce capability strategy is not about selecting items from a shopping list of 'good things to do'. Neither is it about having a succession planning process because everyone says you should have one nor about creating a talent management program because that's what good organizations do.

A workforce capability strategy is about deciding what is required based on business needs. These business needs are usually defined as part of the organization's overall strategy and will vary depending on its products and services, the maturity of the organization, whether it is expanding or contracting, its competitive environment and many other factors such as:

- A change in business direction.
- The introduction of new products and services.
- Changes in technology.
- A potential loss of skills and knowledge due to employee turnover or retirements.
- Outdated workforce skills.
- Limited flow of talent into and around the organization.
- Workforce demographics such as sex and age.
- Skill shortages.
- Poor people management skills.
- Low levels of employee engagement.
- A need to change the organization's culture.

Even within organizations there may be different actions required for different locations, divisions, job groups or demographic groups.

Components of a workforce capability strategy

The aim of a workforce capability strategy is to identify workforce issues and implement prioritized actions to support the successful execution of the organization's strategic objectives. A good workforce capability strategy must provide the answers to the following questions:

- How can I ensure my organization or team has the skills it needs?
- Where do I get the people who have the required capability to do the work?
- How can I retain the skills I have?
- How do I remove excess resources or poor job fits appropriately and fairly?
- How do I know I am managing my workforce effectively?

- How do I ensure people are working to their full potential?
- Can my workforce deliver the organization's strategy?

It is only when all these questions can be fully answered that an organization can be confident of its workforce capability strategy.

Typically, a workforce capability strategy has three parts. These are:

1. **Planning, measuring and reporting:** To identify what needs to be done and to monitor implementation. See Chapter 3 "Planning, monitoring and reporting for workplace capability".

2. **Initiatives to improve or change the working organization** (i.e. improving the effectiveness of the organization's structure, role relationships, systems of work and managerial leadership practices). See Chapter 4 "How to improve the working organization" and Chapter 9 "Cultural Change".

3. **Initiatives to improve workforce capability through specific actions such as:**
    - **Attraction:** To ensure the organization has the ability to attract and select people with the individual capability required to lead and operate the organization. See Chapter 5 "How to attract and select talent".
    - **Retention:** To have skilled and talented people stay longer than they normally would. See Chapter 6 "How to retain talent".
    - **Development:** To ensure current employees have the knowledge, skills and experience required to perform effectively in their role. See Chapter 7 "How to develop workforce capability" and Chapter 10 "How to improve team capability".

- **Removal**: All organizations need the ability to fairly assess and possibly remove people who do not fit the organization's needs. See Chapter 8 "How to remove employees".

The following diagram shows these components together with examples of actions that could be included in a workforce capability strategy. It is not the intent of this diagram to detail every possible strategic initiative for workforce capability but to highlight common initiatives or actions that could be part of a workforce capability strategy.

Workforce capability development strategy

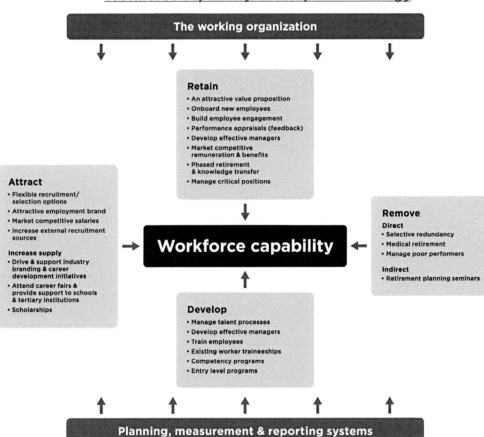

Often, a workforce capability strategy requires the integration of several individual components into one organizational strategy. Examples of these include strategies around employee engagement, organizational culture or safety improvements, which require actions in multiple areas. See Chapter 9 "Cultural change".

The next seven chapters will review each component of typical workforce capability strategies and provide specific information on frequent initiatives.

Key Concepts

- A workforce capability strategy is one component of an organization's strategic planning process.
- A good workforce capability strategy clearly defines workforce requirements to deliver the organization's objectives and the actions required to achieve these objectives.
- Typically, a workforce capability strategy has three parts. These are:
  - ➢ Planning, measuring and reporting: To identify what needs to be done and to monitor how effective implementation has been.
  - ➢ Initiatives to improve the working organization (i.e. improving the effectiveness of the organization's structure, role relationships, systems of work and managerial leadership).
  - ➢ Initiatives to improve workforce capability through specific initiatives such as:
    - o Attraction: To ensure the organization has the ability to attract and select people with the individual capability required to lead and operate the organization.
    - o Retention: To have skilled and talented people stay longer than they normally would.

- o Development: To ensure all current employees have the knowledge, skills and experience required to perform effectively in their role.
  - o Removal: All organizations need the ability to fairly assess and possibly remove people who do not fit the organization's needs.
- Often, a workforce capability strategy requires the integration of several individual components into one organizational strategy.

Tips for Getting Started

1. Review your organization's workforce capability strategy. Does it have initiatives to improve the operation of the working organization?
2. To gain a better understanding of organizational strategy implementation, read the third book in the Leadership Framework Series titled, *Make It Work! How to Successfully Implement Your Business Strategy* by Peter Mills.

Additional information available at www.theleadershipframework.com.au

- Creating a workforce capability strategy – overview.
- Understanding and prioritizing strategic relationships.
- Developing a strategic relationship framework.
- Creating a strategic relationship management plan.
- Building positive strategic relationships.

Chapter 3

Planning, monitoring and reporting for workforce capability

A workforce capability strategy is like any other business strategy. It begins with planning, followed by implementation and then it is monitored and reported to stakeholders.

THE PROCESS TO CREATE a good workforce capability strategy requires an understanding of the organization's strategy and operations, combined with a diagnosis of workplace issues. This diagnosis must not only include the capability of individual employees but also an analysis of the effectiveness of organizational structures, role relationships, systems of work and the effectiveness of managerial leadership practices. The aim of the workforce capability strategy is to support organizational needs. Therefore, human resources professionals need to work closely with senior leaders in the organization.

Planning the workforce capability strategy

The four steps in the business planning process are:

Step 1: Understanding the business

To be able to identify critical issues, human resources professionals must first understand the organization's core business and the current state of that business. Though much of this information will have been gained through day-to-day work and interaction with managers and other employees, additional information needs to be gathered to both support and increase this knowledge. This information will be in:

- Annual business plans.
- The organization's strategic objectives, past and present.
- Forecasts of staffing needs.
- Labor market analytics.

Other useful data will be in:

- Logs of employee issues.
- Employee demographics data.
- Employee turnover and absence rates.
- Employee survey results.

The information gained from all these documents can be used to identify problem areas and will provide background for discussions with senior leaders. Therefore, human resources professionals must analyze all relevant people data so that they can provide insights and 'add value' to the discussions with senior leaders.

Example – Understand the business
In a business, analysis of employee turnover data showed that the average employee turnover in an organization was 10%. When analyzed by years of service, it was found that employee turnover for the first year of service was 33%. After that, most employees stayed for the long term. It was noted, however, that high turnover in the first year of service occurred in only two areas of the organization.

This needs to be discussed with the relevant areas and further analysis may be necessary.

Step 2: Identifying critical workforce issues

With a general understanding of the organizational/divisional strategy and current data on performance and possible people issues, the next step is to arrange meetings with the CEO and senior divisional heads to identify critical issues.

The aim of these discussions is to understand organizational and divisional workforce issues that impact organizational performance and strategy implementation. Discussions need to cover the following topics:

a) Business strategy and direction.
- What are the key business goals over the next two to five years?
- In what ways does successful strategy implementation depend on the outcomes of other business units or other strategic relationships?
- What are your team's strengths that will help achieve the business goals?
- Does the business unit have clarity and a shared understanding of its purpose and direction? How do you know this?
- How do you ensure that goals are effectively aligned and cascaded to those who perform the work?
- How will you know you are successful? How will you measure success?

b) Organizational structure issues.
- Are there too many/too few levels of work from top to bottom of the organization's/division's structure? What is the right number of levels and why?
- Are there any areas within that are currently under/over resourced?

- Is there a need now or in the future to significantly change job types?
- Will people need to change their roles within the organization?
- How effectively do functions/departments/teams work together?
- Are accountability and authority allocated to the correct functions/positions? How are accountability and authority aligned?

c) Systems of work issues.
- What are the key systems of work?
- How do the systems of work support productive work?
- Does each system have a specified owner?
- How are accountabilities and authorities within each system specified? Are these accountabilities and authorities clear?
- Do all systems of work meet the needs of the customer, end user or beneficiary of the system? How do you know this?
- Are all systems of work consistent with legislation, regulations and other corporate policies and standards? When was this last assessed?
- Do systems of work support the organization's values and ethics?
- Do all systems of work have evaluation and control built into the system design? What are they?
- Do all systems of work have a continuous improvement process built into the system design? How do people provide feedback to the system owner?
- Do systems of work support or hinder strategy delivery? What work has been done to align systems to strategy?

d) Managerial leadership issues.
- Are managers held to account for their own personal effectiveness (including their behaviors and ethics)?

- Are managers held to account for the output and behavior of their team? How is this done?
- Do managers build effective teams? How is this assessed?
- Do managers effectively lead their team so that each member is fully committed to, and capable of, moving in the established direction? How is this assessed?
- Do managers continuously improve work processes and methods?
- Are managers effective in leading change?

e) Critical knowledge or skill requirements.
- Are there critical knowledge or skill gaps in your team?
- What knowledge and skills are required for the future? Does the team have these?
- Are there any initiatives in place to retain and build the required knowledge or skills? If so, what are they?
- What additional resources can you draw on to support the skills of your team? How do you know these resources will be available when required?
- Are there any roles in the team that are critical for success?

f) People issues.
- Are there any areas of high employee turnover and/or people whose retention is a concern?
- Are there any areas of poor performance within the team? How are they being managed?
- How well do team members work together? Are there any friction points?
- Does the organization's culture support or hinder strategy delivery?
- Are all employees engaged and performing at the highest level?
- Are there areas of high absence?

- Is the working environment safe? What are your key risks? What are the controls for these risks? How do you know the controls are effective?

Example – Identify critical issues
Following on from the previous example where employee turnover in the first year of service was 33%, possible causes would be discussed with senior leaders. The issue could be related to a number of causes. It could be job design, poor recruitment processes or poor onboarding of new employees. This requires discussion with relevant parties and possibly further analysis.

Step 3: Determining strategic options

When looking at actions for improvement, it is easy to generalize what is required across an organization. However, sections within organizations are often different in terms of:

- Function (e.g. sales vs service).
- Methods of delivery (e.g. internal delivery vs delivery through third parties).
- Demographics (e.g. older workforce vs younger workforce).
- Location (e.g. city vs regional).
- Culture – often determined by the job type and the style of their senior leaders.

Some areas may be male dominated, inflexible and 'rights' oriented, while other areas may be more flexible, have a better gender balance and/or largely deliver their work through contractors. In some cases, the workforce is predominantly based on physical labor while in others it is office based. These differences may require different interventions.

Using the information from the discussions with senior leaders, a 'heat map' can be created that identifies issues in each area. These can then be organized into categories to assess possible larger actions. This will provide a complete picture of organizational requirements.

Workforce capability heat map (example)

Workplace Issue	Category	Area A	Area B	Area C	Area D	Total organization
Work between core functions and corporate specialists not effectively aligned	Organizational structure	x	x	x	x	x
Management of contractors	Knowledge and skills		x			
Managing leave liability	Systems of work	x	x	x	x	x
Employee turnover in first year of service	Systems of work/ managerial leadership	x			x	x
Poor workplace safety systems – unclear ownership	Systems of work			x	x	
Role of manager is not clear	Managerial leadership	x	x	x	x	x
Managers do not build effective teams	Managerial leadership	x	x	x	x	x

Using a heat map helps to organize thoughts, as it separates organizational issues from issues that only impact one area. With this information actions can be prioritized. For example, in the table above, some issues are organization wide, while others, such as the management of contractors, do not require an organizational approach.

Example – Determine strategic options

After reviewing the heat map, it was determined that one of the critical issues, employee turnover in the first year of service, was a critical issue for the organization. Although it was not an issue in every division, the impact was significant for the organization as a whole. Furthermore, onboarding processes were inconsistent across the organization.

Step 4: Deciding and defining initiatives to achieve strategic outcomes

The final step in the planning process is to select initiatives to be implemented. Be careful not to create a large list of 'priority items'. Agree with the CEO and divisional leaders on what is critical to do now and what can be left for later years; otherwise the plan could become overwhelming and little will be achieved. Simultaneously, hold conversations with the human resources leadership team and HR specialists to assess the HR team's ability to support the proposed initiatives.

When priorities are agreed on and clearly defined, then specify the actions required to achieve the initiative and any impediments to implementation.

Once selected, each initiative will require measures to monitor progress. It is important for selected measures to monitor both outcomes and drivers of performance. These are often called lag and lead measures. Outcome or lag measures focus on results at the end of a time frame while driver or lead measures focus on items that drive the achievement of an objective. Balancing outcome and driver measures ensures early warning of things going off track.

Examples of each type of measure are shown in the table.

Outcome Measures vs Driver Measures

	Type of measure	
	Outcome Measure (lag)	**Driver Measure (lead)**
Purpose of measure	To focus on the performance results at the end of a time period or activity, i.e. was the objective achieved?	To measure intermediate processes, activity or behavior that lead to achieving an objective
Example	• Employee engagement level (staff survey result)	• Number of managers trained
Strength of measure	• Usually objective and easily captured	• More predictive in nature • Allows organizations to adjust actions and behaviors toward improved performance
Weakness of measure	• Outcome measures reflect success of past, not current, activities and decisions	• Based on hypotheses of cause and effect • Often difficult to collect supporting data

Each initiative must not only have a measure, it must also be assigned a target to define the desired level of improvement required.

The four main methods of setting targets are:

- Derived from the objective.
- Comparison to a benchmark.
- Incremental improvement from the previous period.
- Establish a baseline and define targets in the future.

An example of each method is shown in the table below.

Methods of Target Setting

Target setting method	Objective	Measure	Target Current year	Next year
Derived from objective	Increase annual revenue to $41,000	Annual revenue	$40,000	$41,000
Comparison to a benchmark	Achieve benchmark performance for customer satisfaction (90%)	Industry benchmark	80%	90%
Incremental improvement from previous period	Reduce defects rate by 1%	Percent of defects	5%	4%
Establish baseline and define targets over time	Improve employee engagement score by 5%	Complete staff survey (to establish a baseline)	Establish current (baseline) level	Baseline plus 5%

Once priorities for action are identified, agreed on and approved, implementation can commence.

Example – Define initiative to achieve strategic outcome
After reviewing the possible causes of high employee turnover in the first year of service, it was decided that poor onboarding was the major cause, and therefore:
The HR team will create and implement a new onboarding process, develop manager checklists for onboarding and create an online portal for new employees by (date). Outcomes will be assessed using the following measures and targets:

- *Percentage employee turnover in first year of service – 15% by (date)*
- *Percentage of onboarding questionnaires completed by new employees – 90%*
- *Percentage of managers completing the onboarding checklist – 95%*
- *Percentage of employees attending corporate onboarding programs – 95%*

Note that these actions are to be placed in the divisional managers' and HR division's business plans.

Implementing the workforce capability strategy

There are three actions required to implement the workforce capability strategy:

i. Organizational alignment.
   a) Assign accountability for the delivery of each initiative.

   Each initiative requires an owner with the necessary accountabilities and authorities for delivery.
   b) Align the organization for success – structure, systems of work, accountability and managerial leadership.

   For each initiative, the working organization must be reviewed and, if necessary, adjusted to support workforce capability strategy implementation. Effective workforce strategy implementation requires:

   - Organizational structure and role relationships to be aligned, with clear accountability and authority, and with role relationships clearly defined to enable roles to work together – see *Typical Accountabilities and Authorities for Corporate Human Resources Functions* in Chapter 4 "How to improve the working organization".

- Relevant systems of work (i.e. policies, procedures, forms, information and communication technologies) to be aligned and communicated to coordinate and direct the new work. See Chapter 4 "How to improve the working organization".
- Management practices to be aligned and communicated to coordinate and direct the new work. See Chapter 4 "How to improve the working organization".

ii. Cascading of initiatives and related tasks.

Each initiative then needs to be cascaded down the organization for effective implementation. Cascading the strategy is a continual process of engaging employees in the strategy by breaking up the complex work into less complex tasks. These tasks are then allocated to each employee, together with the appropriate accountability, authority and necessary resources to complete each task. By breaking up the work and allocating tasks down the organization, strategy becomes linked to day-to-day work.

In the end, successful cascading of the strategy requires every employee to know what they are expected to deliver and how. Specifically, they must know:

1. Where are we going?
   (What is our direction? What are our priorities? What do we need to do to be successful?)
2. What's my role?
   (What is my part in this?)
3. How will my performance be measured or judged?
   (What does success look like? How effective have I been in delivering on my commitments?)

iii. Monitoring and reporting on plan implementation.
Monitoring and assuring the strategy is the final step in strategy implementation. Monitoring and assuring workforce strategy occurs in three ways:

a) Day-to-day processes to monitor and assure strategy implementation.

If cascading the strategy was performed effectively, then the workforce capability strategy will be integrated into the performance planning process as goals and tasks. These goals are assessed as part of a manager's ongoing performance effectiveness reviews of team members, where managers identify any problems or impediments to achieving tasks. This is part of effective managerial leadership.

b) Strategy review meetings.

Strategy review meetings are held to discuss implementation of the workforce capability strategy and its related initiatives. These meetings involve all members of the leadership team, with input from initiative owners and relevant managers with more specific functional expertise. Attendees conduct a high-level overview of strategy implementation. They assess the progress of strategy implementation and the causes and sources of implementation issues. They also recommend corrective actions and assign accountability to resolve issues. Often a separate strategy review meeting is required for each objective as in-depth discussion may be needed.

c) Strategy assessment meeting.

While poor strategy implementation has its own issues, so does implementing a wrong or an out-of-date strategy. A workforce capability strategy is a set of hypotheses about cause and effect relationships.

It is based on information and judgments made at a point in time. The business environment, however, is continually changing, and judgments and assumptions can be wrong or outdated. Strategic plans need to be adaptable and flexible, so they can respond to changes in both the internal and external environments. Therefore, the leadership team should put the whole organization's strategy, including the workforce capability strategy, under full review at least once a year. This is done at a strategy assessment meeting.

Therefore, the purpose of strategy assessment meetings is not to track initiatives. It is to review the organization's strategy and assess if the strategy is still valid and if the strategy will be achieved by the initiatives and, if not, to determine corrective action. The leadership team must test, validate or modify the hypotheses embedded in the strategy; that is, does the strategy remain valid in light of the new knowledge, information, opportunities and changes to the environment?

Furthermore, the leadership team needs to assess if completion of approved initiatives will lead to the achievement of the strategy as planned. If not, are additional initiatives required and/or is an initiative to be modified or cancelled?

In conclusion

At the end of the workforce planning process, senior leaders should be able to answer the following questions:
- What are the human capital implications of the organization's strategic decisions?
- How ready is the workforce to execute on strategic priorities?

- What changes are needed to execute on strategic priorities?
- What actions are we taking?
- Who is accountable for their delivery?
- How will we know we have been successful?

Key Concepts

- The process of creating a good workforce capability strategy begins with an understanding of the business strategy and key workforce issues.
- The four steps in the business planning process are:
  - ➤ Understanding the business
  - ➤ Identifying critical workforce issues
  - ➤ Determining strategic options
  - ➤ Deciding and defining initiatives to achieve strategic outcomes.
- There are three actions required to implement the workforce capability strategy:
  - ➤ Organizational alignment.
    - Assign accountability for the delivery of each initiative.
    - Align the organization for success – structure, systems of work, accountability and managerial leadership.
  - ➤ Effective cascading of goals and tasks.
  - ➤ Effective monitoring and reporting.
    - Day-to-day processes to monitor and assure strategy implementation.
    - Strategy review meetings.
    - Strategy assessment meetings.
- At the end of the workforce planning process, senior leaders should be able to answer the following questions:

> What are the human capital implications of the organization's strategic decisions?
> How ready is the workforce to execute on strategic priorities?
> What changes are needed to execute on strategic priorities?
> What actions are we taking?
> Who is accountable for their delivery?
> How will we know we have been successful?

Tips for Getting Started

1. Review your current workforce capability plan. Were stakeholders involved in setting priorities?
2. Have items in the workforce capability plan been prioritized?
3. What are the key measures and targets for your workforce capability strategy? Who is accountable to achieve outcomes? Are these the right roles?
4. Assess how effective your organization is in monitoring workforce strategy implementation. How could you improve it?

Additional information available at www.theleadershipframework.com.au

- Overview of the strategy implementation process.
- Defining the strategy.
- Aligning the organization for strategy deployment.
- Cascading and deploying the strategy.
- Monitoring and assuring the strategy.
- Accountability for strategy development and implementation.
- Tools and resources - Why strategy implementation often fails.

Chapter 4

How to improve the working organization

Understanding and managing the impacts of the working organization on employee effectiveness is essential for productive work.

WHILE MANY ORGANIZATIONS TURN TO TRAINING PROGRAMS as a first step to improve workforce capability, the area to review first should be the working organization. This is because the root cause of many people issues is not the lack of individual capability but rather organizational dysfunction. This dysfunction can be sourced from:

- The employee's direct manager.
- The organization's strategy, structure, role relationships and systems of work.

These factors are shown in the diagram below.

Factors affecting employee personal effectiveness

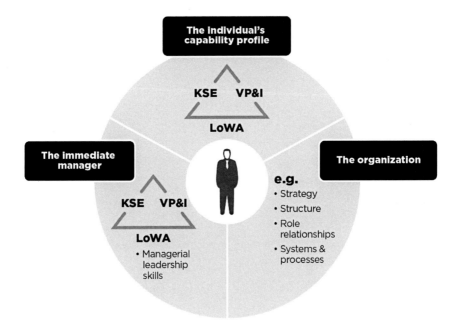

Direct (immediate) manager impacts

An employee's immediate manager impacts an employee's performance effectiveness every day. To be effective an employee's immediate manager:

i.   *Must have the individual capability to perform their role effectively.*
     This means they must have the knowledge, skills and experience (KSE) to do their role, they must value the work, including the people work (VP), and be free of inhibiting behaviors (I). The manager must also have a level of work ability (LoWA) to be able to operate at one level of work above their direct reports, so they

can add value to their work. If the manager cannot add value to their team members' work, then team members will become dissatisfied and seek third party support from other managers, human resources or unions, thus undermining the manager-team member working relationship.

ii. *Must effectively deliver managerial leadership to team members.*

Firstly, managers need to have a clear understanding of what they are accountable to do and what authorities they have to do it. This understanding goes beyond the technical and programming aspects of a role and extends to the requirements of managing people. The Leadership Framework provides a clear definition of managerial work.

The role of the manager is to *achieve the business goals set for them, while providing an environment that allows their team to be effective and satisfied with their work while developing their full potential.*

Specifically, managers are accountable for:
- Their own personal effectiveness.
- The output and behavior of their team.
- Building and leading an effective team, so that each member is fully committed to, and capable of, moving in the established direction.
- Continuous improvement of work processes and methods.

Managers deliver these accountabilities by effectively conducting the performance management sequence. This sequence starts with effective role design, followed by selection for the role, then induction of the individual into the role. It continues while the individual is working in the role. Each part of the process has a different emphasis with the same goal: having fully loaded roles filled with people capable of doing their work. This sequence is shown in the diagram below.

The performance management sequence

Role: Role design establishes the role in the organization. It sets out its business purpose and objectives, its accountabilities and authorities, and its working relationships with other roles.

Select: Selection identifies and appoints an individual whose capability is judged to best suit the capability requirements of the role.

Induct: Induction familiarizes those selected with the work of the role, its relationships with other roles and the incumbents in those roles, the systems of work including the policies and work processes relating to the role, an overview of the typical tasks, the current priority tasks and the performance requirements of the role.

Assign: Effective task assignment is the foundation of getting work done and a condition for individual performance effectiveness.

Assess: After a task is assigned, the manager then monitors the individual as he or she progresses in the work, providing feedback on progress and how effectively the individual is working.

Reward: The intent of rewarding and recognizing team members is to create conditions where all employees are in a position to see that the organization is a meritocracy – a place where people are paid fairly based on their performance effectiveness.

Develop: Development in the role follows naturally from effective task assignment and completion, as the manager reviews the work and the individual's effectiveness in executing the work. The manager creates opportunities to coach the individual on how to be more effective. This may involve helping the individual see better ways to solve problems, run meetings, collaborate with others, comply with rules and policies or better use the company's resources.

Secondly, managers must be able to build strong manager-team member working relationships. They do this by:

- Addressing the work interests of team members. Managers must answer the four questions all employees have:
  - ➤ Where are we going?
  - ➤ What's my job?
  - ➤ How will my performance be judged?
  - ➤ Where am I going? (answered by the manager once removed).
- Creating an inclusive culture. Keeping team members informed on what is happening in the business unit and providing them with opportunities to be involved in the decision-making process.
- Providing role clarity. Ensuring team members understand their role requirements. This extends beyond the tasks in the position description. It includes the broader accountabilities of all employees for their work, and how they are expected to work with their manager, their team and others in the organization.

- Providing a safe working environment. Managers cannot build strong manager-employee relationships or expect productive work in an unsafe work environment. Providing a safe working environment goes beyond the control of physical hazards and includes providing a workplace free from bullying, harassment and discrimination.

Providing effective managerial leadership both supports and enables the individual capability of team members. Without effective leadership, work will become confused and team members frustrated. This may lead to reduced personal performance, poor behaviors, workarounds, or duplication of work.

Organizational impacts

To create a working environment that both enables and supports productive work, organizations must provide all employees:

a) Clear business purpose and direction.
For the working organization to operate effectively, people in the organization must know where their organization/function/department is heading and their role in this. Without clear direction, the context of people's work will be confused and unproductive work will occur. There will be a lack of prioritization of projects and a waste of time, effort and resources. There will be confusion on what is important to the organization, and therefore what is important to people's day-to-day work. This resultant confusion will impact the ability of people to perform their role.

It is the role of the CEO and leadership team to provide organizational direction, and every manager at every level must provide direction for their team.

Having clear direction is not a training issue. It is a managerial leadership issue.

b) Effective structures, functions, roles and role relationships. An organization's structure provides the shared understanding of accountability and authority that exists between people whose work is aligned and integrated with other roles to deliver the organization's products and services in line with the strategy.

Clear roles, with defined working relationships, provide the basic rules of engagement for people to work together. Such rules include who needs to work with whom, who makes the decisions and who carries out the work. A common problem for many organizations is the lack of integration of work between core functions, such as sales, service and manufacturing, and specialist corporate functions, such as finance and human resources. Typical issues are:

- What are the specialist corporate functions vs the core functions accountabilities and authorities for work?
- How do corporate specialist functions and line manager accountabilities and authorities integrate?

When designing organizational structures, line manager roles and specialist function roles should be complementary. They should not be in conflict. What is required is a clear understanding by all parties of the accountabilities and authorities of these complementary relationships.

An example of aligned accountabilities and authorities is outlined in the table below for a corporate human resources function.

Typical Accountabilities and Authorities for Corporate Human Resources Functions

Element	Corporate Human Resources	Line manager roles (CEO, executive team, managers)
Strategy	• Develop and recommend the workforce capability strategy	• Decide organization's workforce capability strategy • Input to the workforce capability strategy • Decide cross-functional alignment
System of Work Design	• Design and recommend the system of work required for the workforce capability strategy	• Input to the design • Decide the system
System of Work Use	Deliver service to enable managers to use the system in their own areas, for example: • Provide specialist services (e.g. recruitment) • Provide training services • Provide advice on the use of the system • Coordinate activities to enable system use	• Lead the implementation, using the system as authorized • Initiate services within the agreed context of the function or system • Review and assure performance to system (by own team) • Decide trade-offs within system's limits
Governance: Control, Monitor, Audit	• Collate and analyze data on compliance and quality • Recommend improvements • Recommend corrective action • Report against measures • Action authorized system changes	• Provide data for reporting • Provide feedback on system effectiveness • Decide corrective action • Implement corrective action in own teams

Using the example of a workforce capability strategy, to operate effectively the corporate human resources function should be accountable to develop the organization's workforce capability strategy, as they are the technical experts in this area. The corporate human resources function must then recommend the workforce capability strategy to the CEO and leadership team. The authority to decide if it is the right strategy for the organization is performed by the CEO with input and feedback from the full leadership team.

Following this, as the corporate human resources function is accountable to develop the strategy, it is logical that they must also be accountable to design the systems of work to support implementation of the approved strategy.

Strategy implementation must be led by each manager for their own team, in line with corporate requirements. The role of the human resources function is to provide advice and support to line managers.

Lastly, as the human resources function designs the strategy and systems of work, it is logical they also be required to monitor and audit the implementation of the strategy.

Failure to specify the accountabilities and authorities for specialist roles creates the environment for conflict and has predictable consequences:

- Blurred accountabilities and authorities will result in duplication of effort and/or gaps in delivery. As a result, office politics may emerge, with the related poor behaviors undermining the organization's effectiveness or undermining its values.
- Work will be performed by the wrong roles. Time and resources will be wasted in "sorting out" the work.
- Workarounds and unauthorized systems of work will be developed as people will still want to achieve their objectives outside the authorized system of work

(e.g. creating local spreadsheets to collate data for reporting).

- The human resources manager will not be able to hold team members to account for their personal effectiveness as they will likely be trying to deal with ineffective working relationships and may not have clear authority to act.
- Employees will need to rely on the goodwill of their peers to get work done.
- Many meetings will be held with little outcome.

All this impacts the ability of people to work together and hinders workforce strategy implementation. The issue is not about relationship management. It is about providing clarity through organizational/role design to allow people to use their individual capability.

c) Productive systems of work.

Systems of work consist of the organization's policies, procedures, processes and information and communication technologies. They enable roles to work together to deliver the organization's products and services.

Systems of work:
- Facilitate work across functions, across teams and within teams.
- Provide the *standardizing* methods and boundaries for work.
- Align people and work with legislation, social norms and the organization's values.
- Allow the leadership team to monitor and verify that the organization's purpose and strategy are being achieved in accordance with its cultural, ethical and moral standards.

Systems of work are a key component of the day-to-day working environment for most employees. People not only work in the system, but they also interact with it, and it interacts with them. As systems of work critically influence the ability of people to do their best work, they critically impact workforce capability. Therefore, systems of work need to support each person to deliver their required outcomes.

Common conflict spots in the design of a system of work are where:
- Handover points are not clear.
- Incorrect or incomplete inputs are received from others that delay or impair work.
- The system does not do what it is supposed to do.
- The system is adjusted with little or no consideration for those who work in the system or those who rely on the system's outcomes.
- Accountabilities and authorities for the system or within the system are unclear.
- The work outputs are not used or not trusted.

Once again, these are organizational issues that impact workforce capability.

To resolve this problem, all systems of work must be fit for purpose. Therefore, as a minimum, all systems of work must include the following eight design principles:

i.   All systems of work must have a designated system owner.
For any system of work, the owner should be the cross-over manager for all users of the system. This is because the cross-over manager is the only role that:
- Can work across all related processes within the system, with the authority and experience to identify and implement necessary changes.

- Has the authority to engage the whole team to understand and agree on the principles of the system, to assure it is fit for use and then to hold them accountable for input, implementation, and review.
- Can understand and integrate all the feedback loops and time-delayed effects in the system.
- Can ensure the system of work is used effectively across the whole area of application.

Having the cross-over manager as the systems owner ensures the whole system is considered when it is designed or when changes are made. In this way, decisions can be made on what is best for the total system of work, not just to satisfy one person or department.

ii. All systems of work must be designed to meet the needs of the customer, end user or beneficiary of the system.
As systems exist to deliver specified outputs for customers, end users or beneficiaries of the system of work, these people/roles must be identified and their needs understood and specified. This is important so that:
- The quality, quantity and timeliness of system outputs can be determined.
- Stakeholders can be advised or consulted when the system is altered or is to cease operation.

iii. All systems of work must be consistent with legislation, regulations and other corporate policies and standards.
Systems guide peoples work therefore, they must be consistent with legislation, regulations and the other corporate policies that reflect the

organization's standards and values. For example, the development of a sales or production system must be consistent with other relevant organizational systems, such as the People Management System, the Safety Management System, the Environmental and the Quality Management System. Failure to do so would not only put the organization at risk, it would be inconsistent with organizational requirements and would inevitably lead to conflict with those who work in other systems of work.

iv. The design of all systems of work must include the specification of working relationships.

Working relationships must be established between roles, not people. Establishing clear role relationships enables work to be done and disagreements to be resolved. In establishing working relationships, the system's designer must specify the accountabilities and authorities for each role that uses the system of work. This will ensure clarity on issues around the system's inputs, processes, outputs and feedback mechanisms.

v. All stakeholders must be engaged in the development and use of the system.

All the system's stakeholders must be consulted on its development and use. Where required, a user reference group can be created to provide input. This will not only ensure appropriate input and an appropriate level of consultation in the system's design, but it will also build trust and reduce the potential for conflict in the future.

vi. All systems of work must equalize treatment of employees, unless there is a business-related reason not to equalize.

When looking at different systems of work, it is important to understand their intent. Is the intent to differentiate or to equalize? Systems of equalization treat people the same way. They do not differentiate between an operator, a manager or the CEO. An example of this is a safety system. Irrespective of your position, title or rank, if you enter certain work sites, you must wear a hard hat and other required personal protective equipment. Systems that equalize promote organizational trust and fairness.

Systems of differentiation treat people differently; they distinguish between roles. For example, some roles are paid based on commissions, while others are not.

All systems of work should equalize unless there is a clear work-related or business-related reason not to. If there is no such reason for a system that differentiates, the system and the associated managerial work are likely to be seen by employees to be unfair and can be expected to diminish mutual trust in the organization. Unfair systems drive non-compliance and dysfunctional behavior.

vii. All systems of work must have evaluation and control built into the system design.

Systems can only be maintained as authorized and productive systems if control and audit work is effectively established. Controls assure the correct use of the system.

Where possible, measures must also be established. These measures must be directly related to the purpose and outcomes of the system. They need to consider all aspects of the output: quality, quantity, cost and timeliness.

Example of Controls and Measures for a Recruitment System

Control	Measure	Period
Example 1: Recruitment Quarterly dashboard	Cost per hire (cost) Time to fill (timeliness)	Post-recruitment review Quarterly report
Example 2: Recruitment End of probation period questionnaire	Quality of hire against position description and key values/behaviors (quality)	3 months after hire (end of probation)

viii. All systems of work must have a continuous improvement process built into the system design.

All systems of work must be designed with feedback mechanisms. The system's owner/custodian is accountable to ensure suggestions are considered and changes authorized and communicated.

Using the systems of work design principles in this chapter will not only improve workforce capability, but it will also support strategy implementation, improve productivity, organizational trust and the quality of the working environment, reduce unnecessary conflict and aid in employee retention.

In summary

All aspects of employee performance are impacted by the working organisation i.e. the employee's direct manager, the organization's strategy, structure, role relationships and systems of work. This is not a training issue; it is a managerial leadership issue as the work environment is created by an employee's direct manager and the organization's leadership team.

Key Concepts

- The root cause of people issues may not be their lack of individual capability but rather organizational dysfunction. This dysfunction can be sourced from:
  - ➢ The employee's direct manager's own capability and managerial practices.
  - ➢ Unclear organizational direction, the organization's structure, role relationships and systems of work.
- The role of the manager is *to achieve the business goals set for them, while providing an environment that allows their team to be effective and satisfied with their work while developing their full potential.*

- Specifically, managers are accountable for:
  - ➢ Their own personal effectiveness.
  - ➢ The output and behavior of their team.
  - ➢ Building and leading an effective team, so that each member is fully committed to, and capable of, moving in the established direction.
  - ➢ Continuous improvement of work processes and methods.

- Managers deliver their accountabilities by effectively conducting the performance management sequence:
  - ➢ Role design.
  - ➢ Selection.
  - ➢ Induction.
  - ➢ Assigning and assessing work.
  - ➢ Development.
  - ➢ Reward.

- In addition, managers must be able to build a strong manager-team member working relationship by:
  - ➢ Addressing the work interests of team members.
  - ➢ Creating an inclusive culture.
  - ➢ Providing role clarity.
  - ➢ Providing a safe working environment.

- Managing workforce capability requires all aspects of the working organization to work effectively. This work environment is created by the direct manager and the organization's leadership team.
- To create a working environment that both enables and supports productive work, the organization must provide:
  - Clear business purpose and direction.
  - Effective structures, functions, roles and role relationships.
  - Productive systems of work.

Tips for Getting Started

1. Review the role of the manager in your organization. Are the people managerial leadership accountabilities and authorities clearly defined?
2. When reviewing the performance of your team, assess how you, as a manager, impact team performance effectiveness.
3. Review the main system of work in your department. Does it help or hinder work performance? Why?
4. Are the accountabilities of specialist corporate functions such as finance and human resources clearly defined? Do specialist corporate role accountabilities and authorities complement line roles or is it unclear who is accountable for financial or people issues?
5. To gain a better understanding of the concepts of the impact of the working organization on each employee's personal effectiveness, read the second book in the Leadership Framework Series titled, *Don't Fix Me, Fix the Workplace: A Guide to Building Constructive Working Relationships* by Peter Mills.

Additional information available at www.theleadershipframework.com.au

- The working environment.
- What is work?
- How managers align work.
- Manager role, accountabilities and authorities.
- Acting manager role, accountabilities and authorities.
- Supervisor/team leader role, accountabilities and authorities.
- Employee role, accountabilities and authorities.
- Specialist/cross functional roles, accountabilities and authorities.
- Manager once removed roles, accountabilities and authorities.
- Project manager role, accountabilities and authorities.
- Committee role, accountabilities and authorities.
- Principles for organizational design.
- Accountabilities and authorities for organizational design.
- Description of levels of work.
- Accountabilities and authorities for cross team work.
- Typical accountabilities and authorities for corporate specialist functions.
- Systems of work roles, accountabilities and authorities.
- Principles for design of a system of work.
- Process for designing/reviewing systems of work.
- Systems of work and culture.
- Tools and resources – Systems of work accountability map.
- Tools and resources – Systems of work control document template.
- Tools and resources – Example: System of work control document people management system.
- Tools and resources – Example: System of work control document selection.
- Tools and resources – Systems of work effectiveness scan.

Chapter 5

How to attract and select talent

*A critical component for building
workforce capability is the ability to
attract and select capable employees to
operate the organization.*

ATTRACTING AND SELECTING high quality staff is a critical component for any workforce capability strategy. Not having the right 'raw material' compromises the ability of organizations to achieve their objectives.

The purpose of any attraction and selection strategy is to attract high quality candidates who meet the job requirements and to select, on a merit basis, the candidates who best fit the roles.

Other outcomes required from the selection system are:

- A fair and equitable selection process.
- The people selected are a good fit to the organization's values.
- Following a reasonable settling in period, there are no surprises to either the immediate manager or the selected employees with regard to the work of the

role, the employee's 'fit-to-role' or the performance expectations of the role.
- Roles are filled within time and cost specifications.

Common attraction and retention strategies

Two key initiatives of an attraction and selection strategy are:
- Creating an employment brand.
- Improving the selection process.

A. Creating an employment brand.

Having more and better qualified applicants for a role makes the selection of a good employee more likely. However, organizations are often challenged to distinguish themselves in the marketplace. One way to do this is to communicate to potential employees what the organization offers. All organizations have an employment brand, whether specified or not and whether managed or not. It is therefore important to ensure the right messages are getting to potential employees.

Employment branding enables organizations to communicate their employment value proposition, ensuring they attract the type of talent that fits with their corporate values and direction, thereby increasing the likelihood that attracted talent remains with the organization for the long term. By communicating the employment brand, organizations effectively compete for talent with other organizations in the market for similar types of employees.

Effectively managing and communicating an employment brand has other benefits. These include:

- Ensuring consistency in recruitment advertising across the organization.

- Presenting a unified image of the company across business and regional units.
- Providing candidates with an accurate and clear vision of company culture and values.
- Retaining critical employees.

It also can assist organizations in becoming an employer of choice.

i. What are the ingredients of an employment brand?

Simply, an employment brand is comprised of what the labor market values and what the organization delivers and communicates to the market. An employment brand can also be part of an organization's employment value proposition (EVP), which includes why people stay with an organization. Whether creating an employment brand for attraction or retention, or both, it is important to understand that the aspects for attraction are those that potential employees can see from outside the organization, while aspects for retention also include things that only current employees can see from the inside. For example, most organizations attract new employees with good remuneration or location, as these can easily be communicated as part of the recruitment process. The quality of an organization's management, however, is more difficult to communicate but is seen and felt by employees in the organization, so acts as a factor for retention. One of the requirements of an employment brand is to communicate attributes that the organization has but are difficult to see from the outside.

The diagram below outlines the primary drivers of attraction and retention.

Drivers of attraction & retention

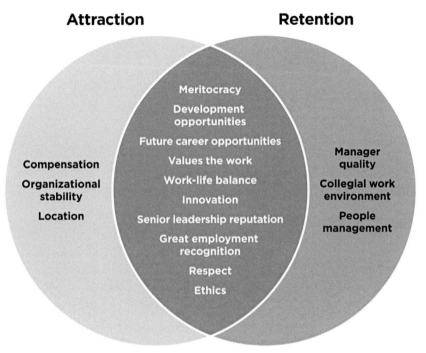

From Corporate Leadership Council

ii. Process to create an employment brand.
The process to create an employment brand has seven steps.

1. Define the purpose of the branding exercise.
Decide why the organization needs an employment branding strategy. What is its purpose? Is it for specific types of roles or all roles? Is it just to attract potential employees or is it part of a broader EVP to retain employees?

2. Research and analyze brand options.
   Define the unique value proposition of the organization. What does or can the organization offer that the labor market values (e.g. work-life balance, industry leadership)?

   This research and analysis includes:
   - Reviewing the drivers of attraction and retention.
   - Conducting focus groups.
   - Conducting employee preference surveys.
   - Reviewing HR survey information.
   - Brainstorming possible options.

3. Select the brand.
   Select brand attributes that best fit the organization's needs. Attributes selected need to be in areas where:
   - The organization has a strength.
   - The organization has a competitive advantage.
   - There is alignment with the organization's overall strategy/objectives.
   - The cost to implement is relatively low.
   - The brand elements are realistic and deliverable.

   When selected, create a tagline that communicates the essence of the brand (e.g. 'Make a Splash' at Sydney Water) and test proposed brand on key stakeholders (e.g. focus groups, new employees, recruitment organizations).

4. Gain leadership buy-in.
   Present brand to leadership team and gain support and approval where necessary.

5. Create branding material.
   Material will need to be created and/or changed to reflect and communicate the new brand. This includes:

- Promotional materials for career fairs.
- Material for the organization's website and social media.
- Content for new employee inductions.
- Sales brochures.
- Company reports.

All material that goes to, or is seen by, third parties should be reviewed.

6. Launch brand.
   Actions could include:
   - Internally communicating new brand.
   - Externally communicating and leveraging new brand.
   - Marketing the brand at career fairs.
   - Feature brand details on relevant websites and social media.
   - Engage recruitment companies in branding promotion.

7. Maintaining and monitoring the employment brand.
   The employment brand will need ongoing work to maintain, develop and promote. It is a continual process, not just a one-off exercise. Part of this is to ensure the brand is reflected in day-to-day work. Where there is a difference in the brand and day-to-day work experience, then new employees are likely to leave while current employees will be disaffected.
   To monitor the effectiveness of the employment brand, metrics will also need to be created. Metrics could include:
   - Number of applications for roles before and after brand implementation.
   - Number of job offer declines.
   - Number of website visits.
   - Market recognition.

B. Improving the selection process

Many organizations select people solely on their knowledge, skills and experience. This can result in a poor outcome. The purpose of the selection process is to assess the alignment of an individual's capability profile (see Chapter 1 "What is workforce capability?") with the role's requirements.

To be successful a person must:

- Have the *knowledge, skills and experience* (KSE) required to do their role. While selecting a person without the full knowledge, skills or experience will impact their ability to perform their tasks, it is not always essential that a candidate have all the requirements of the role. Sometimes judgments need to be made, as knowledge, skills and experience can be learned or acquired over time. Sometimes high potential employees may be appointed to gain new knowledge, skills and experience.

  In making a judgment on suitability, the manager needs to select a candidate who has a KSE level that at least meets the minimum requirements of the role or has the capability to do so within a short period of time.

- *Value* (V) the work they are being hired to do. Where an individual does not find value or enjoyment in a particular kind of work, they are unlikely to be able to sustain effort over time to excel in their role.

  The interview process should review employment history, voluntary work, study and hobbies to assess if candidates 'value the work'.

- Be free from *inhibitors* (I); that is, personal characteristics which get in the way of working and reduce the employee's effectiveness in the role. These may include:

chronic problems with interpersonal relationships, aggression, disabling extremes of temperament and drug and alcohol dependency.

During selection, the manager (and the manager once removed) must assess the extent to which personal inhibitors may be present, what potential there may be for the candidate to overcome these inhibitors and what risk any inhibitor may pose to job performance. The careful checking of references from people or organizations where the applicant has previously worked will assist in this assessment.

- Have a *level of work ability* (LoWA) matched to the most complex task in the role; otherwise, they will not be able to solve the problems of the role and may not even understand that there is a problem. Matching an individual's level of mental processing ability with the complexity of tasks in a role is a minimum requirement to work effectively as training will not improve job performance.

  Assessing an individual's LoWA is best done through discussion of the complexity of tasks performed in previous roles and cross-checking the performance of these tasks with previous managers and organizations.

When a person's KSE, VP&I and LoWA match the role requirements, the person feels satisfaction in being able to do their role well. When there is a mismatch between an individual capability profile and role requirements, it is detrimental to both the organization and the individual. It means that the work required in the role is most likely not being done effectively and that the person in the role feels either underutilized or overstretched and may have poor self-esteem as a result. A general principle is that people will grow or shrink their role and tasks to the level of work in which they are most comfortable operating. This applies to all roles at all work levels. The more complex the role (e.g. managing director or general manager), the greater the risk to the delivery of organizational outcomes.

i. Accountability for selection.

As managers are accountable *to build and lead an effective team,* it naturally follows that managers are accountable to select members for their team. However, during the selection process, both the manager and the manager once removed (MOR) hold an equal right to veto any appointment to a manager's team. The reason for this is that:

- The manager is accountable for team performance; therefore he/she must be satisfied that the selected candidate can perform the role.
- The MOR is accountable for developing capability for future business needs and for ensuring that the long-term view is considered. For example, the MOR may be aware that the manager is retiring or transferring to another role in 12 months' time and therefore may be looking for a replacement.

Therefore, both the manager and MOR must be comfortable with the selection and must agree, so they can both meet their respective accountabilities.

Often it may be appropriate to have others on a selection panel where they can 'add value' to the selection process. This may include technical specialists or a recruitment specialist. However, in every case, the manager must exercise his/her managerial authority (with the MOR) in deciding the selection. Panel members other than the manager and the MOR should have accountability and authority limited to advising them on the selection.

ii. Maintaining and monitoring recruitment process.
To ensure the effectiveness of the recruitment system is maintained, audit and feedback mechanisms need to be built into the system of work for selection.

Systems performance measures should also be created to monitor the effectiveness of the selection system. Measures of performance could include:
- Manager satisfaction with the recruitment process.
- New employee satisfaction with the recruitment process.
- Voluntary separation rate (<1 year tenure).
- Involuntary separation rate (<1 year tenure).
- Average number of days taken to fill vacancies.
- Average recruitment cost per employee.

Key Concepts

- Attracting and selecting high quality people is a critical component for any workforce capability strategy. Not having the right 'raw material' compromises the ability of organizations to achieve their objectives.
- The purpose of any attraction and selection strategy is to attract high quality candidates who meet the job requirements and to select, on a merit basis, the person who best fits the role.
- Two of the key initiatives of an attraction and selection strategy are:
  - Creating an employment brand.
  - Improving selection processes.
- An employment brand is comprised of what the labor market values and what the organization delivers and communicates to the market. It enables organizations to communicate their employment value proposition, ensuring they attract the type of talent that fits with their corporate values, thereby increasing the likelihood

that attracted talent remains with the organization for the long term.

- The process to create an employment brand has seven steps:
  - ➤ Define the purpose of the branding exercise.
  - ➤ Research and analyze brand options.
  - ➤ Select the brand.
  - ➤ Gain leadership buy-in.
  - ➤ Create branding material.
  - ➤ Launch brand.
  - ➤ Maintain and monitor the employment brand.
- The purpose of the selection process is to assess the alignment of an individual's capability profile. To be successful a person must:
  - ➤ Have the *knowledge, skills and experience* (KSE) required to do their role.
  - ➤ *Value* (V) the work they are being hired to do.
  - ➤ Be free from *inhibitors* (I), that is, personal characteristics which get in the way of working and reduce the employee's effectiveness in the role.
  - ➤ Have a *level of work ability* (LoWA) matched to the most complex task in the role.
- During the selection process, both the manager and the manager once removed (MOR) hold an equal right to veto any appointment to the team. The reason for this is that:
  - ➤ The manager is accountable for team performance; therefore he/she must be satisfied that the selected candidate can perform the role.
  - ➤ The MOR is accountable for developing capability for future business needs and for ensuring that the long-term view is considered.
- To ensure the effectiveness of the recruitment system is maintained, audit, feedback and measurement need to be built into the system of work for selection.

Tips for Getting Started

1. Do a survey of new employees to assess why they chose to join the organization? Use this information in future job advertisements.
2. Review how your organization selects employees. What are the criteria for selection? Is it KSE only or do you look at LoWA and VP&I?

Additional information available at www.theleadershipframework.com.au

- Designing effective roles.
- Resourcing options.
- Selecting the right person for a role.
- Manager role, accountabilities and authorities.
- Acting manager role, accountabilities and authorities.
- Supervisor/team leader role, accountabilities and authorities.
- Manager once removed role, accountabilities and authorities.
- Creating an employer brand.
- Tools and resources – Sample position description template.
- Tools and resources – Matching a person to a role.
- Tools and resources – Example of how to determine your employer brand.
- Tools and resources – Example of employer branding material.

Chapter 6

How to retain talent

*Retaining talented employees is an
essential component for any workforce
capability strategy.*

RETAINING TALENTED EMPLOYEES is essential for any organization
to both operate effectively and to achieve business goals.

The purpose of a retention strategy is to have skilled and
talented people stay longer than they normally would, as no
one stays forever. Furthermore, organizations should not be
encouraging people to stay if it would be better if they left the
organization. A retention strategy needs to balance the need
to retain people with an understanding that organizations
cannot provide growth and career opportunities or
continuing employment for everyone. Retention strategies
only work where there is a mutual benefit for both parties –
the employee and the organization.

Common Retention Strategies

As discussed in Chapter 4 "How to improve the working
organization", the working organization not only impacts

workforce performance, but it also impacts employee retention. Therefore, improvements in the function and operation of the working organization will directly impact employee retention. Initiatives to improve the working organisation include:

- Improving the quality of management.
- Improving systems of work.
- Improving organizational trust.

Other common initiatives to improve workforce retention include:

- Improving remuneration management.
- Recognizing and rewarding good performance.
- Onboarding new employees.
- Managing critical positions.

A. Improving the quality of management

As every employee has a manager, the quality of management is a key issue for retention of employees. The saying that 'people join organizations and leave managers' is substantially true. Improving the quality of management and the quality of the manager-team member working relationship not only improves productivity, but it also improves the quality of the work environment and the retention of employees.

Initiatives to improve manager quality are covered in Chapter 7 "How to develop workforce capability" and initiatives to improve team capability are covered in Chapter 10 "How to improve team capability".

B. Improving systems of work

Systems of work are a key component of the day-to-day working environment for most employees. Where systems of work are well designed and aligned with requisite managerial leadership, their influence will be highly beneficial, as effective systems of work enable productive work, support constructive working relationships and supports retention.

If, however, a system of work is poorly designed, it may be misused, and its influence will be counterproductive. Furthermore, unfair systems drive non-compliance and dysfunctional behavior. Poorly designed or unfair systems of work not only impact work outputs, but they also create unnecessary work and have the potential to cause frustration, friction and conflict. The effective design and deployment of systems of work are therefore essential for constructive working relationships and employee retention.

Initiatives to improve systems of work were covered in Chapter 4 "How to improve the working organization".

C. Improving organizational trust

People tend to stay in organizations where they are treated fairly and trust the organization 'to do the right thing'. Systemic trust, like organizational culture, is built through the interaction of organizational structures, including role design, systems of work and managerial leadership.

i.   Role of organizational structure
     The design of an organization's structure and roles builds trust by clearly defining the required working relationships. This design provides the shared understanding of accountability and authority that exists between people whose work is aligned and integrated to implement the organization's strategy. The basis for **collaboration** is built on role design, clear definition of accountabilities, authorities and role relationships. (See Chapter 4 "How to improve the working organization" and Chapter 10 "How to improve team capability".)

ii. Role of systems of work.

The senior leadership team builds trust into the design and deployment of its systems of work, including its rules, regulations, policies, procedures and symbols. These systems of work create custom, practice, traditions, beliefs and assumptions. Systems of work reinforce what is valued in the organization and what is valued by the senior leadership team. Unfair systems, and the managerial work associated with this, will diminish organizational trust. While trust and fairness must be built into all systems of work, it is essential for people management systems. In relation to trust, the most important principles for system design are:

- They are consistent with legislation, regulations and other corporate policies and standards.
- All stakeholders are engaged in the development and use of the system.
- They equalize treatment of employees unless there is a business-related reason not to equalize.
- They have evaluation and control built into the system design.
- They have a continuous improvement process and feedback mechanisms built into the system design.

See Chapter 4 "How to improve the working organization".

iii. Role of the manager once removed (MOR).

One way organizational trust is improved is by formally integrating the role of the manager once removed (MOR) into the people management system. The manager once removed is each individual employee's manager's manager.

The manager-once-removed relationship

Nearly every employee in an organization has a MOR. Even at the general manager/vice president level, the chair of the board can act as a MOR.

While most organizations have not specifically identified the role, accountabilities and authorities of MORs, they often build them into the systems of work for people management, such as employee appeals or dismissals. However, this lack of formal identification of MOR accountabilities and authorities is a gap that can cause relationship issues among managers, their direct reporting team members and their own manager.

To enable organizational trust, the following accountabilities from The Leadership Framework should be built into the role of the manager once removed.

a. Ensure the consistency and quality of leadership for their employees once removed. They do this by:
   - Linking vertical and horizontal role relationships to ensure collaboration and alignment.
   - Coaching their direct report managers on their leadership effectiveness.
   - Shaping the workplace culture and setting expectations of behavior for all managers in the business unit.
   - Reviewing managerial decisions of their direct reports as part of performance assessment.

b. Ensure fair treatment. They do this by:
   - Providing objectivity for decisions affecting their managers team.

- Ensuring consistent application of policies across the business unit.
- Deciding appeal outcomes.

c. Build capability for the future. They do this by:
  - Bringing a wider perspective of the organization to identify future opportunities and role requirements.
  - Designing organizational structures for the employees once removed.
  - Assessing the potential of the employees once removed for current and future roles (see Chapter 7 "How to develop workforce capability").
  - Deciding on promotion/demotion/dismissal of employees once removed.

d. Integrate the work of their team of teams. They do this by:
  - Setting the context for work of the business unit.
  - Establishing systems of work that integrate the end-to-end processes of the business unit.
  - Ensuring their managers collaborate constructively to achieve the overall plan of the business unit.
  - Aligning work across teams.

Building these accountabilities, with the appropriate authorities, into the organization's systems of work will increase organizational trust and fairness. For example, building the requirement for the MOR to review a direct manager's assessment of their team members' performance effectiveness review or remuneration review improves the fairness of the system. This in turn improves trust in the organization.

Integrating the role of the MOR into the people management system ensures the consistent application of policies and practices, brings greater transparency and strengthens accountabilities and their fulfillment throughout the organization. It also brings a wider perspective to people management issues – all of which create systemic trust.

iv. Role of the manager.

Managers build trust and strong manager-team member working relationships through the effective delivery of their role. This means managers must:

a. Demonstrate capability in their role.

To demonstrate capability in their role, managers need:

- Specific knowledge, skills and experience. This goes beyond the technical and programming aspects of the manager's role. It includes the people management skills.
- To value their work.
- A level of work ability to add value to the work of their team.
- The absence of negative behaviors. If a manager demonstrates extremes of behavior, such as aggression, bullying, harassment or drug and alcohol dependency, these behaviors will overshadow the good work a manager does and will reduce their effectiveness in the role. Trust will be diminished and working relationships negatively impacted.

b. Demonstrate trust-inducing behaviors.

In relation to behaviors, a lot of research has occurred over the years to determine the behaviors required by leaders. In examining this issue through the lens of The Leadership Framework, we find there are four behavior requirements to be a successful manager. These are:

- Honesty
- Integrity
- Respect for others
- Collaborative behaviors

There are specific reasons for this list. These reasons are:

1. To perform their role effectively, managers must *build a strong, two-way, trusting working relationship* with each team member. This working relationship can only be built if there is trust, and trust cannot be developed without **honesty, integrity** and **respect** for others. These behaviors are essential ingredients to build trust. Without these behaviors, there can be no trust; without trust, a strong manager-team member working relationship cannot develop.

2. Managers must work with others to be successful. They have working relationships with their own direct team and their own manager. They also work across teams, with other managers and with people in specialist roles. They must work **collaboratively** with them to achieve the organization's goals. This basis for collaboration is built into the organization's structure and role design, with a clear definition of role accountabilities and authorities, and uses the organization's systems of work. Furthermore, to be effective, managers must not only understand the roles of others in the organization, they need to **respect** those roles and the people in them.

3. All other so-called behaviors are learnable skills, such as 'how to give feedback', or are behaviors resulting from failures in the operation of the working organization (e.g. unclear accountabilities, authorities or role relationships in the organizational structure or role design) or the outcome of ineffective managerial leadership.

It is important to note that:

- In delivering these behaviors, managers should use their personal style. Often organizations seek to change the personality of managers. When this occurs, it usually fails as people are not able to maintain these changes over long periods of time. Alternatively, they seem fake to their team. Everyone is an individual and people need to work together within boundaries and guidelines, but they do not have to be the same. They do, however, have to continually demonstrate the behaviors of honesty, integrity, respect and collaboration.

- Demonstrating these behaviors does not mean that managers will build trust. These behaviors are necessary, but not sufficient, to create the trust required to build the strong manager-team member working relationships required for productive work. Good behaviors and interpersonal skills have limited value however, in a workplace and/or working relationship which is otherwise flawed in its design or subject to ineffective leadership. While the use of good interpersonal skills (by everybody) will assist in establishing more constructive behaviors and provide some 'social glue', they are not enough on their own.

c. Provide a safe place to work.

Managers must provide a safe working environment for their team. This not only includes providing a safe physical environment but also an environment free from bullying and harassment. Besides any moral or legal obligation to do so, managers cannot build the trust required for strong manager-team member working relationships or expect productive work in an unsafe work environment.

d. Consistently and fairly apply systems of work.

Managers must consistently and fairly apply the organization's systems of work. Consistent application of good managerial practices and systems of work builds trust. Every time a manager fails to apply a consequence for breaches of a system of work, the manager automatically creates new wider boundaries for their team members' work performance. If the manager applies consequences to some team members and not to others, questions of favoritism or victimization will arise. This undermines trust.

Furthermore, if a manager personally fails to demonstrate use of a system, this action is in effect 'approving' non-compliance for team members as they continually evaluate the manager's behavior in all interactions. For example, if a policy prohibits team members from sharing passwords that access computer applications, but then the manager shares his/her password when information is required, this undermines both the system and the manager. It reduces trust.

e. Continually engage their team.

All employees want to be part of an organization's success. However, to do so they must personally be engaged in the organization. To ensure team members are engaged, managers must continually address the four key questions that all employees can be expected to have. These are:

- Where are we going? (What is our direction? What are our priorities? What do we need to do to be successful?)
- What's my role? (What is my part in this?)
- How will my performance be judged? (How am I measured?)
- Where am I going? (What is my future in the company? This last question is answered by the team member's manager once removed.)

These questions are often answered through the organization's systems of work. For example, the answer to the question, 'What is my role?' is contained in position descriptions. The answer to 'How will my performance be judged?' is in the performance appraisal system. However, managers must continually set the context for team members through both formal and informal processes on a day-to-day basis. Keeping the focus on these four questions engages team members in their work and builds trust.

f. Create an inclusive culture.

An inclusive culture can only happen when team members are kept informed by their manager on what is happening in the business unit and are provided with opportunities to be involved in the decision-making process. This is a genuine two-way process that does not merely take into account the input of team members but also deliberately involves and engages them as a means to build trust, motivation and to ensure an optimum outcome.

This does not mean that an inclusive culture is a democracy where decisions are reached by consensus or vote. It means that team members are encouraged to have an input and are heard. The manager, however, as he/she is accountable for the output of the team, makes the final decision.

g. Provide role clarity.

Role clarity, with clear accountability and authority, builds individual confidence and esteem. It generates trust in the system of work. Managers therefore, must ensure team members understand their role requirements, including the role's boundaries. This allows people to apply their knowledge, skills and experience to achieve outcomes. Role clarity enables people to exercise judgment in making decisions. It enables them to use their capability. Role clarity enables empowerment. (See "Effective role design" in Chapter 10 "How to improve team capability".)

Role clarity, however, extends beyond the tasks in the position description. It includes the broader accountabilities of all employees on how they are expected to work with their manager, their team and others in the organization. In organizations, all employees are obliged to deliver the outputs required of their role and use the resources and processes specified by the organization. Expectations, however, go beyond this. There are standards or expectations of behavior on how people are to interact to achieve business outcomes.

While many organizations have values, few clearly articulate how people are to work together. They may value teamwork or collaboration and use phrases such as, 'We all have to work together,' 'We need to collaborate more effectively,' or 'We must have constructive behaviors.' However, few organizations define what this looks like, and even fewer hold their people to account for delivery.

In The Leadership Framework, all employees have an accountability to do their best and to work together to achieve business outcomes. This work is defined, so that the behaviors of honesty, integrity, respect for others and collaboration are embedded in the accountabilities for all employees. For example, collaboration is embedded in the requirement to 'work productively together'. When implemented, these expectations become the social norms for the organization. These requirements are expanded in the following table.

Expectations of All Employees

Expectation	Required Behavior
Fulfill commitments made	• Deliver in full and on time all their output commitments and expect the same of others. This includes commitments made across the organization to other individuals or departments • Uphold the organization's values • Under no circumstances should they 'surprise' their manager on the delivery of output commitments
Bring their full capability to work	• Apply their knowledge, skills and experience fully and effectively • Exercise their discretion to deliver outcomes fully and appropriately • Try different ways to achieve objectives even in difficult circumstances • Work cooperatively with others to solve problems and share information within the context of the role • Work within set policies, systems and procedures — refer to a higher level where appropriate • Accept and adapt to change
Continue to develop their performance effectiveness	• Work to improve their personal effectiveness in their role by actively participating in people management processes such as goal-setting and development

Expectations of All Employees (continued)

Expectation	Required Behavior
Provide their manager with feedback	• Actively engage with their manager when tasks are assigned • Look at ways to improve by providing feedback to their manager on tasks, systems and processes used • Refer problems that cannot be resolved to their manager for assistance • Immediately notify their manager if they are unable to achieve assigned task output (quantity, quality, time or cost)
Work together productively	• Work together to solve problems within the context set by their manager • Persuade each other to act in a way that facilitates their work, to accommodate each other's needs as far as possible without changing or compromising their accountabilities or agreed/allocated objectives • Do what is right for the function and the organization, even when this may cause a potential difficulty for their area • If there is disagreement, they act as their manager would want them to, before escalating to their manager • If agreement cannot be reached, they must escalate to their immediate manager who will either clarify the context or make a specific trade-off decision

Expectations of All Employees (contined)

Expectation	Required Behavior
Limitations	• Should not tell each other what to do
	• Should not stop each other from taking action
	• Should not fight about who is right, but focus on the issue
	• Should never speak negatively about their colleagues
	• Team members are not accountable for each other's work and do not make judgments about each other's personal effectiveness. This is the role of the manager

Adapted from Elliott Jaques

The delivery of these expectations will reduce the causes of conflict and enable people to work together constructively. They build trust.

These expectations, combined with clear role authorities such as 'to provide advice', 'monitor' and 'give service' and as part of role design, describe what collaboration looks like. (See Chapter 10 "How to improve team capability".) Where the rules for interaction are not clearly specified, they will develop regardless.

v. Maintaining and monitoring organizational trust.

To ensure organizational trust is maintained, audit and feedback mechanisms need to be built into the related system of work.

Monitoring organizational trust can be done informally through feedback to team members or formally through the organization's performance management process. It can also be done through organizational or team surveys. Metrics could include employee surveys that assess:

- The application of people management policies.
- The manager- team member working relationship.
- The effectiveness of MOR interactions.

D. Improving remuneration management

It is well recognized that employees who receive differential rewards, based on a fair criterion, tend to work more effectively and stay longer with an organization. For retention purposes, the intent of the remuneration system is to create conditions where all employees are in a position to see the organization as a meritocracy – a place where people are paid on the basis of work performance, not seniority, technical skill or membership in a favored group.

i. The importance of fairness.

In relation to retention of employees and pay, the question is not necessarily 'How much?' but 'Is it fair?' The ideal state is where employees can say, 'I feel I am working at a level suited to my capability, and I am fairly rewarded for that work. I feel I am contributing to the success of the organization, and I can see a clear link between my performance and my remuneration.'

An effective remuneration system does not mean lucrative remuneration. While high levels of remuneration are effective in attracting new employees and retaining current employees, employees on low salaries can be highly engaged while those on high salaries are not. People paid at equitable levels feel satisfied, and pay is not raised as an issue. Remuneration does, however, need to 'feel fair' to all employees.

In relation to fairness, when making comparisons on pay, people ask three questions:

1. How am I paid compared to others who do my job in other organizations? (i.e. is there external equity?) This comparison focuses on what employees in other organizations are paid for doing the same or similar roles. The fact that management views its employees as 'well paid' compared with those of other organizations does not necessarily correspond with employees' beliefs. Employees have different information and make different comparisons than management.

2. How am I paid compared to others at the same or higher levels in my organization? (i.e. is there internal equity within the pay system?) This comparison focuses on what employees within the same organization but with different roles are paid. Employees make comparisons with lower level roles, roles at the same level (but with different skill requirements) and roles at higher levels. Internal equity is achieved when the pay structure is differentiated primarily by the level of work, that is, by a role's complexity.

3. Am I rewarded for my effort? (i.e. are people paid differentially?) This relates to being recognized and rewarded for 'my performance effectiveness' when compared to others in similar roles. To ensure pay 'feels fair':

   - Remuneration needs to be linked to an objective criterion that is known to the individual employee (i.e. quantity, quantity and/or time requirements).
   - Access to the reward must be clearly understood. The rules and triggers must be simple and clear.

- The outputs required for the differential reward must be within the person's control. Team members can only be held accountable for their own effectiveness. They cannot be held accountable for the impacts of other people, things that could not be planned or things that are outside their control (e.g. a sudden and unexpected fall in the economy or an economy that can produce outstanding results with little effort from the individual).
- The link between contribution and personal effectiveness must be clear. While this is a matter for judgment by the manager, the evaluation should be fairly based on what a person has done.

Having strong direct links with the reward system, however, does carry risk. For example:
- Does the organization have the right measures and targets?
- Does it have reliable data for the measures?
- Could unintended and unexpected consequences arise from the way the targets for the measures are achieved?
- Did the employee's manager support or hinder the employee's achievement of their objectives?
- What are the impacts of the working organization (i.e. its structure and systems of work and managerial leadership) on the employee's personal effectiveness?

ii The effectiveness of bonus systems.

Currently there is widespread and increasing use of bonuses as a tool for driving organizational performance improvement, especially at the executive level. It should be noted that there is no conclusive research proving that bonuses are effective at improving organizational performance. This approach to remuneration management often reflects, in part, the views of the CEO or the board. But do they work?

While there appears to be universal acceptance of the importance of differential pay based on an individual's performance effectiveness, there are legitimate arguments around the usefulness of individual bonus systems. This debate centers on the basic beliefs about human motivation and work. Are people basically lazy? Do they need to be urged to work? If an employee's pay is established properly as 'feels fair pay', then why have a bonus system?

Proponents of bonus systems argue that bonuses:

- Are an effective way of getting people to focus on key objectives.
- Are a powerful tool for sending a message and aligning people with organizational objectives.
- Are an effective method of rewarding superior performance (even where they do not see it necessarily as a means of driving performance).
- Do not lock in salary costs and pay increases because the incentive must be re-earned.

Critics argue that:

- If employees are engaged to do their best (i.e. to work to their full potential), then it is illogical to attempt to reward them for greater performance.
- Employees can only be held accountable for doing their best in working toward their goals. As an employee's performance effectiveness is impacted by the performance effectiveness of their own manager and other organizational

factors, such as structure and systems of work, they cannot be fully held to account for outcomes.

- In the absence of disciplined task assignment and other related managerial practices, no bonus pay system can be made fair. Better results can be gained with improved goal setting, as poor goal setting may result in goal underachievement, despite the best efforts of the employee, or goal overachievement with little effort.

- External influences, such as market conditions and supplier issues, are outside the employee's control and can significantly impact outcomes.

- Bonuses can cause friction and a sense of injustice and can undermine team solidarity.

- Employees become too focused on the incentive at the cost of the long-term success of the organization.

- Required outcomes are not always clear, can change or are not as expected. What happens if the strategy was wrong or needs to be adjusted mid-term?

- Bonus schemes can be compromised more than a standard pay system because employees quickly come to see them as disconnected with reality. This causes cynicism and possible 'gaming' of the bonus scheme (e.g. the employee bidding down targets against the manager bidding them up).

- There are additional administration costs for bonus systems.

- Often executives are being rewarded for short-term operational work rather than long-term strategic work. While each level of work in an organization is performed over different time frames, most bonus systems are annually based and don't hold executives to account for long-term sustained growth via multi-year performance targets.

There may be an argument that reasonable long-term incentives are suitable for some executive levels, but only if they relate to goals set according to level of work and time span of task, as outlined in the table below.

Level of work	Type of work	Time span	Level of employee
V	Business direction	5–10 years	CEO/Managing director
IV	Strategic delivery	2–5 years	General manager
III	Operational direction	1–2 years	Functional manager
II	Team leadership	3 months–1 year	Frontline manager

Furthermore, many employees do not like individual bonus systems. The main reasons are:

- They may not be reflected in their superannuation, pension or retirement benefits.
- It is difficult to plan individual finances around a bonus.
- Financial institutions often do not consider bonuses in their criteria for loans.
- They can be withdrawn at any time.
- Outcomes can be influenced by factors outside their control.
- Goals may be just missed, but they lose their entire bonus.
- The flow-down effect from their manager pushing to achieve their goals (i.e. 'I already work hard now. How much harder do you want?').

The establishment of any reward system requires an understanding of people in a work environment. The Leadership Framework believes that people are naturally motivated to work, that work is something people value and people come to work to do their best. If a person is hired to do their best work, why do they need more motivation? If a team member's performance drops, then it is an issue for the manager (requiring assessment of the cause and an intervention). The cause may be outside the control of the team member. These causes include organizational structure, systems of work, the capability of the employee's manager and unclear task assignment. If this is accepted, then it is difficult to punish a person and not give them a bonus because of this.

iii. Maintaining and monitoring remuneration management. Consistency in remuneration management is achieved through good salary system design and implementation, part of which includes a manager once removed (MOR) calibration process. Ensuring fair treatment is an important part of the role of the MOR in developing and sustaining an environment of trust and confidence in the system of management.

To ensure the effectiveness of the remuneration system is maintained, audit and feedback mechanisms need to be built into the system of work. Metrics could include:

- Compensation compared to market.
- Internal relativities.
- The fairness of the remuneration system.
- Profit return on every dollar invested in employee remuneration.
- Compensation expenses as a percentage of total operating expenses.
- The proportion of the organization's operating expense comprised of total employee remuneration.

E. Recognizing and rewarding good performance

Recognizing good work is a key way to engage and retain employees. Recognition and reward go beyond just pay, and a big budget is not needed to recognize people for their effort. Effective recognition can cost nothing. The cheapest, easiest and quickest reward is a verbal 'thank you' for a job well done.

While managers should always be looking for reasons to reward or recognize team members for their performance effectiveness, such recognition must be linked to key outcomes such as goals, behaviors or contribution to the team's success. Reasons to recognize and reward team members include:

- Achieving a goal
- Finishing a major project
- Working long hours to finish an urgent project
- Demonstrating required behaviors
- Outstanding customer service
- Community service

For recognition to be effective, managers need to understand the work of the team member and their contribution. Recognizing team members for work they have not done, or have not contributed to, can demoralize other team members.

Recognition is most powerful the closer it occurs to the event being recognized. To give full impact to recognizing an achievement, the manager must follow three simple steps:

Step 1: Thank the team member: expressing gratitude is key to recognizing someone and making them feel appreciated.
Step 2: Describe what the team member did: ensure the team member understands why they are being recognized so they are more likely to repeat the behavior in the future.

Step 3: Explain how the team member's actions added value: describe how the action helped you, the team and/or the organization.

There is no one way to recognize team members as different things work for different people according to their different preferences. The key is to make the reward personally relevant to the person receiving it. Giving a gym membership to someone who does not want it is pointless. Examples of possible rewards and recognition include:

- Professional development.
- Contributions to favorite charities.
- Gift vouchers – they let the employee pick their own gifts.
- Flowers, chocolates, cakes, books, movie tickets.
- 'Thank you' notes.
- Complimentary company products.
- Time off.
- Additional leave.
- A morning tea with the team.
- Formal and informal recognition at an organizational event.

It is really up to the imagination of the manager. However, it must be within the organization's policy provisions.

Maintaining and monitoring employee recognition systems

To ensure the effectiveness the employee recognition system is maintained, audit and feedback mechanisms need to be built into the system of work. Metrics could include:

- An employee survey that assesses how and how often managers provide feedback to team members.
- An audit on the operation and use of corporate-wide recognition systems.

F. Onboarding new employees

When looking at retention strategies, an often overlooked area is the onboarding of new employees. Failure to adequately induct new team members can lead to underperformance, lack of engagement and loss of motivation and may result in the employee choosing to leave the organization shortly after starting. I have worked in organizations where some sections had an employee turnover in the first year of services of 32%. After implementing an effective onboarding program, this declined to 10% within 18 months.

Onboarding starts when the successful applicant accepts the offer of employment and continues until the employee is performing effectively in the role.

When a new team member starts, it is an important early opportunity for managers to begin applying correct managerial practices and to build the strong manager-team member working relationship required for productive work.

Good onboarding results in:

- A strong, two-way, trusting and productive working relationship focused on achieving the business objectives.
- Faster performance effectiveness in the role.
- Full employee engagement.
- Minimal employee turnover in the first year of service.

i. The onboarding process.

   When new team members join a business unit, gaps may exist between the requirements of the role and the new team member's knowledge, skills and experience. In these circumstances, and as part of induction into the role, managers must draw up a plan, in conjunction with the new employees, to close these gaps over time. This development plan is expressly aimed at making sure the new team members are effective in their role as soon as possible. It ensures they earn their keep as quickly as possible and feel satisfaction in doing this. It also means they are working towards their full potential.

Induction for new team members usually occurs in two parts: a corporate induction and a role induction. The corporate induction provides some of the essential information for new employees. For the organization, the corporate induction should cover:

a) Who are we and why do we exist? Who are our stakeholders?
b) What we do and where are we heading?
c) How do we do it?

The role induction must, at a minimum, cover:

a) The role of the business unit and how it fits within the organization – the business unit's objectives, tasks and projects.
b) How the role fits within the business unit.
c) What work the new team member will do – typical tasks and the current priority tasks for the role.
d) The systems of work applicable to the role which include the policies and work processes relating to the role.
e) The role's relationship with other roles and the incumbents in those roles
f) How the team member will be provided feedback.
g) How the team member will be assessed – the performance requirements of the role, the manager's expectations of what a good job looks like when the role is being performed satisfactorily.

ii.   Maintaining and monitoring onboarding systems.
      To ensure the effectiveness of the onboarding system
      is maintained, audit and feedback mechanisms
      need to be built into the system of work. Metrics could
      include:
      - An employee survey that assesses the effectiveness
        of onboarding.
      - Employee turnover in the first year of service.
      - An audit of the operation and use of corporate-
        wide systems.

G. Managing critical positions

Critical position management is a part of an organization's
risk management processes. It is about ensuring roles essential
to the functioning of an organization, both at the strategic
and operational level, are continuously filled with capable
people.

Broadly speaking, a critical position is a role (not a person)
that has a direct and significant impact on the organization's
ability to operate successfully and, if left vacant for a
significant period of time or filled with a person without the
required individual capability, the organization would not
achieve its objectives. A position is labelled critical based on
the position's importance in achieving business goals, not on
the individual who holds it.

The definition of a critical position is defined in line with
the organization's needs. This definition must be specific, yet
applicable across the whole organization. The factors on
which to base an organization's critical position program
include:

- Strategic impact: The role has a significant impact
  on strategy achievement and would be difficult to
  fill internally or externally given the scarcity of the
  skills required to perform the role. For example, if

the business strategy is to improve the quality of its products and services, then roles associated with quality assume greater importance.

- Operational impact: The role has a significant impact on revenue, business operations or product development and would be difficult to fill internally or externally given the scarcity of the skills required to perform the role. Operational impact can manifest in a number of ways, including the role's value in providing:
  - ➢ Enhanced customer satisfaction.
  - ➢ Cost reduction.
  - ➢ Improved quality.
  - ➢ Greater efficiency or time to market.
  - ➢ Improved systems and processes.
  - ➢ Improved financial performance.
  - ➢ Product and service innovation.

Due to changing organizational priorities, positions may be identified as critical in one year but not critical the next. For example, a role managing a key strategic project may be critical to establish the project. However, once the project has commenced and others have gained experience working on the project, the project leader's role may no longer be critical for delivery.

A critical position management program aims to:

- Objectively identify critical positions through a facilitated review with business leaders.
- Employ risk management strategies to mitigate the risk of loss.
- Track critical positions and their related risk management strategies.

i. Critical position management process.
    The process to identify and manage critical positions is:

    1. Define precisely what a critical position is for the organization.

2. Gain CEO and executive team support to identify and manage critical positions.
3. Implement the critical position management program:
   - Meet with managers once removed and managers to identify critical positions.
   - Review and validate nominated positions as 'critical'.
   - Create a summary of critical positions.
   - Confirm critical positions with CEO and executive team.
   - Create a risk management strategy for each critical position. Strategies to mitigate risks include:
     - Retention of occupant – signed term agreements, job and salary reviews, individual development plans, flexible work arrangements.
     - Role Reengineering – separate key activities of role and spread these activities across other roles.
     - Succession Plans – identify staff with similar skill sets and develop career paths and development plans to fill critical roles.
     - Technology replacement – move to automate key activities using technology to reduce reliance on individual knowledge.
     - Reporting Lines – realign roles to similar functions to cross skill and increase pool of available employees to fill roles.
4. Gain approval for risk management strategies.
5. Implement risk management actions. If retention of the role's occupant is part of the strategy, complete a 'Retention Risk Assessment'. The aim is to assess the risk of the person holding the

critical position of leaving the organization. Areas to be assessed include compensation, work relationships, work-life balance, job challenge and recognition. A detailed risk mitigation plan should then be created to minimize the loss of talented individuals from the organization.

6. Integrate critical position identification and management into business plans.

ii. Maintaining and monitoring critical positions.

To ensure the effectiveness of the critical position management system is maintained, audit and feedback mechanisms need to be built into the system. Furthermore, critical positions and their risk management strategies should be reported to and reviewed by the organization's leadership team annually.

Measures of performance include:

- The number of critical positions (the lower the better).
- Percentage of critical positions with a risk management plan.

Organizational retention

While each retention initiative will have its own measures to monitor performance and to define success, so will the organization as a whole. Measures for organizational retention include:

- Employee engagement level.
- Employee retention rate.
- Employee satisfaction with managerial leadership.

Key Concepts

- Retaining talented employees is essential for any organization to both operate effectively and to achieve business goals.
- The purpose of a retention strategy is to have skilled and talented people stay longer than they normally would.
- A retention strategy needs to balance the need to retain people with an understanding that organizations cannot provide growth and career opportunities or continuing employment for everyone. Retention strategies only work where there is a mutual benefit for both parties – the employee and the organization.
- Strategies to improve retention can include:
  - Improving the quality of management.
  - Improving systems of work.
  - Improving organizational trust.
  - Improving remuneration management.
  - Recognizing and rewarding good performance.
  - Onboarding new employees.
  - Critical position management.
- Organizations can improve trust by:
  - Improving the effectiveness and clarity of the working organisation – structure, roles and role relationships, systems of work and managerial leadership.
  - Formally integrating the role of the manager once removed (MOR) into the people management system.
- Managers build trust and strong manager-team member working relationships by:
  - Demonstrating capability in their role.
  - Demonstrating the trust-inducing behaviors of honesty, integrity, respect for others and collaborative

behaviors. In addition, there must be an absence of negative behavior.

- ➢ Providing a safe place to work.
- ➢ Consistently and fairly applying systems of work.
- ➢ Continually engaging their team.
- ➢ Creating an inclusive culture.
- ➢ Providing role clarity.
- For retention purposes, the intent of the remuneration system is to create conditions where all employees are in a position to see the organization as a meritocracy.
- In relation to retention of employees and pay, the question is not necessarily, 'How much?' but 'Is it fair?' The ideal state is where employees can say, 'I feel I am working at a level suited to my capability, and I am fairly rewarded for that work. I feel I am contributing to the success of the organization and I can see a clear link between my performance and my remuneration'.
- There is no conclusive research proving that bonuses are effective at improving organizational performance. This approach to remuneration management often reflects, in part, the views of the CEO or board.
- Recognizing good work is a key way to retain employees.
- Failure to adequately induct new team members can lead to underperformance, lack of engagement and loss of motivation and may result in the employee choosing to leave the organization shortly after starting.
- Induction for new team members usually occurs in two parts: a corporate induction and a role induction.
- Critical position management is about ensuring roles essential to the functioning of an organization, both at the strategic and operational level, are continuously filled with capable people.

- Broadly speaking, a critical position is a role (not a person) that has a direct and significant impact on the organization's ability to operate successfully and, if left vacant for a significant period of time or filled with a person without the required individual capability, the organization would not achieve its objectives.

Tips for Getting Started

1. What is your view on the level of trust in your team(s) (i.e. as a manager of a team and as a member of a team)? What can you do to increase the level of trust?
2. Seek clarification of the accountabilities and authorities of the manager once removed (MOR) in your organization. Assess if they are formalized and designed to support productive work. Do they support trust and fairness?
3. What are the 'expectations of all employees' in your organization? How do employees know these expectations and how are they assessed and monitored?
4. Organize an induction of a new employee using the information in this chapter.
5. Define a critical position in your organization.

Additional information available at www.theleadershipframework.com.au

- Tools and resources – Onboarding policy sample.
- Tools and resources – Business unit onboarding checklist and plan.
- Tools and resources – End of probation period questionnaire – Manager.

- Tools and resources – End of probation period questionnaire - New Employee.
- About pay.
- When and how to recognize and reward work.
- Trust, fairness and systems of work.
- Trust and fairness – The role of the manager once removed.
- Ensuring the consistency and quality of leadership.
- Ensuring fair treatment and justice.
- Managing critical positions.
- Tools and resources – Career conversations guide for employees.
- Tools and resources – Career conversations guide for the manager once removed.
- Tools and resources – Critical position identification form.
- Tools and resources – Critical position summary.
- Tools and resources – Retention risk assessment.

Chapter 7

How to develop workforce capability

Developing the individual capability of employees is a continual and essential process for business success.

ALL ORGANIZATIONS NEED to ensure their people have the individual capability to perform their role. Organizations, however, are in a constant state of change - changes to technology, changes to products and markets and changes to the way work is to be performed. Furthermore, people leave, new people are employed, and people are promoted or transferred to new roles. All of this requires continual people development actions to ensure the organization has the knowledge, skills and experience necessary to operate effectively.

The aim of employee development is to ensure all employees have the knowledge, skills, experience and behaviors required to perform their role effectively in a constantly changing work environment.

Common workforce capability development strategies

Three of the key workforce development initiatives are:
- Talent identification and development.
- Manager development.
- Skills/competency programs.

A. Talent identification and development

Talent identification and development is on the agenda for most organizations. The aims of talent development programs are to:

- Accurately identify talented individuals
- Improve retention and performance of talented individuals.
- Build a pipeline of capable individuals who can move into key roles.
- Actively engage all of the organization in talent identification and development.

i. Defining talent.
    Many organizations make the identification and management of talent overly complex. They find it difficult to define talent, and they confuse talent management with succession planning. Sometimes they divide talent into nine boxes and try to manage each group separately. The unintended outcome is they spend a large amount of time and resources on talent identification, with very little real development happening. 'Identified talent' then become disengaged and leave the organization. It is important, therefore, to be clear on exactly what talent is and who is accountable to develop identified talent.

    A simple definition is that talent is 'a person who has the individual capability to work at a higher level in an organization'. However, while this definition is technically correct, organizations often waste time and money creating talent programs for individuals who do not want higher roles or who are not engaged in the organization.

When defining talent, the three questions to be answered are:

- Does the person have the individual capability for higher roles?
- Does the person aspire to perform a role at a higher level?
- Is the person engaged in the organization?

a. Does the person have the individual capability for higher roles?

Using the definition of individual capability in Chapter 1 "What is workforce capability?", individual capability is defined as a person's:

unique combination of knowledge, skills and experience (KSE) to deliver the accountabilities of their role, their level of work ability (LoWA) and valuing the work sufficiently to release energy and commitment to sustain high performance, with an absence of personal, disabling temperament (VP&I).

Therefore, to be identified as talent, a person must:

- Have a LoWA equal to that of the next level or have the potential to acquire it in the near future. This has to be the first criteria to be satisfied for talent identification as, if a person's LoWA is lower than that required for the role, they will not be able to solve the problems that arise in the role and cannot therefore meet the role requirements. *No amount of training will assist.*
- Value the work of higher level roles. If a person does not value the work, *no amount of training*

or development will assist. Developing people for higher level roles where they have no interest in the work will fail.

- Have at least the minimum level of KSE to perform a role at a higher level or be able to attain it over a reasonable time. *Managerial coaching and training can be effective in improving a person's knowledge, skills and experience.*

Finally, the person must not demonstrate extremes of behavior, which get in the way of working. *Such behaviors should be eliminated before promotion to the next level.*

b. Does the person aspire to perform a role at a higher level?

To be considered as talent for development, a person must also aspire for a role at a higher level. This is not a person who just values the work; it is someone who wants the higher level role. Personal aspiration may be driven by financial rewards, a desire for overall advancement or the opportunity to have additional influence. Aspiration, however, may be limited by work-life balance requirements such as not wanting to work the longer hours required, having a young family or being the sole parent. As these are personal issues, it is up to the individual to decide. Furthermore, individual circumstances may change over time. Alternatively, organizations may be able to make some adjustments to fit individual needs.

It is not up to the manager to make assumptions about a person's aspirations. Decisions can only be made after discussion with the individual.

c. Is the person engaged in the organization?

Does the organization want to develop people who are not committed to it and do not intend to stay? This can be a vexing issue for organizations. The answer will depend on how the organization views development. Where organizations have limited funds, these funds may be better utilized for the development of others.

If, however, the view is that all people should have the opportunity to develop their capability to the fullest, then the answer is 'yes' (provided they meet the other criteria for talent). It may be that the development of the person will increase their engagement in the organization and their intent to stay.

Therefore, every organization should define what 'talent' looks like in their organization based on their business needs.

ii. Accountability for talent identification and development.

In The Leadership Framework, managers are accountable to develop team members for their current role only. They are not accountable for the identification and development of future capability. It is the manager once removed (MOR) who is accountable for developing capability to meet future business needs, and therefore, for talent pool development (see Chapter 6 "How to retain talent"). The reasons MORs have accountability for talent management are:

- They are interested in developing a replacement for their current managers.
- They are more willing to 'release' or 'transfer' employees within their team of teams for development.

- They have a broader view of the organization, so they can see what opportunities are available across their 'team of teams'.
- They have a level of work ability at least two levels above their manager's team members. Therefore, they are more able to recognize individuals who can work at the next level.

The different accountabilities for development between the immediate manager and manager once removed are summarized in the table below.

Immediate manager		Manager once removed
What are they accountable for?		
Personal effectiveness management		Talent pool development
What are they accountable to do?		
Maximizing performance effectiveness in the current role		Development of future potential
What do they do?		
Facilitate the alignment of individual employee activities with the strategic objectives of the business through task assignment, feedback, coaching, training and development, recognition and rewards		Provide opportunities for the development of employees to their maximum potential to meet current and future business needs

What is assessed?

The individual's ability to work in a specific role at a given level at the present time

The maximum level at which an individual can work in a role at the present time, and/or a future time, given that they value the work and possess the necessary skilled knowledge.
It is a function of an individual's raw LoWA.

What is the main process used?

Coaching – the ongoing working dialogue between a manager and a team member in which the manager helps the team member to increase his/her personal effectiveness in his/her current role

Mentoring – the process where the MOR helps the person to understand her/his full potential and how that potential might be developed to achieve career growth in the organization

The role of human resources is to create and manage the systems of work to support the process and to assist and advise managers at all levels on talent identification and development.

iii. The talent management process.

The talent management process has four key stages:
- Talent identification.
- Development.

- Risk management.
- Monitoring and review.

a. Talent identification.

To identify talent, managers once removed (MORs) should meet, at least annually, with their staff once removed (SOR) and discuss career plans with SOR. In these meetings the MOR needs to gain an understanding of the SOR's aspiration and engagement in the organization.

With input from the direct manager, the MOR must form a clear judgment about the SOR's current potential – that is, what level of work and which kinds of roles the SOR could occupy now (if he/she has full knowledge, skills and experience, fully values the work and has no disabling extremes of temperament) and the SOR's future potential for the next two to five years.

b. Development.

With these judgments established, and after discussion with the immediate manager, the MOR should reach an agreement on an appropriate career development program for the SOR. The MOR must determine what is possible and desirable from the organization's point of view.

Outcomes of any meetings with the SOR must be discussed with the SOR's manager, and development actions placed in the individual's personal development plan.

For his/her part, the SOR must decide what he/she wants to do and can commit to. The actual development work might be carried out by the immediate manager or through special projects. However, the decision on development opportunities rests with the MOR. All learning and development experiences are aimed at getting the individual job ready to follow the preferred career path as soon as the opportunity presents itself.

There are two types of development that need special care to ensure the manager- team member working relationship remains intact. These are:

- Transfer decisions – MORs determine when they want individual SORs transferred as part of their career development or to fill a role that has become vacant. The MOR discusses this with the SOR's manager before making a decision. The immediate manager can also recommend transfer where she/he sees the person might be suitable for a particular role, but the MOR makes the decision.

- Acting opportunities – Acting in a role is a key development opportunity. It provides the MOR with an opportunity to form a view on potential candidates who may be able to meet a future business need. The decision as to who acts in a role is that of the manager once removed. For example, the decision as to who acts in a general manager role should be that of the CEO, not the general manager. It is the CEO who selects the SOR to fill the role temporarily from all of his/her SORs.

c. Risk management.

A retention risk assessment should be completed for each person on the talent program. The aim is to assess the risk of the person leaving the organization. Areas to be assessed include compensation, work relationships, work-life balance, job challenge and recognition. A detailed risk mitigation plan should then be created to minimize the loss of talented individuals from the organization.

d. Monitoring and review.

Monitoring progress occurs at two levels: by MORs and by the organization. MORs ensure their direct reporting managers perform, where applicable, their talent development activities.

The organization monitors talent through effective systems of work using appropriate measures. Examples of such measures include:

- retention of top talent
- percentage of risk management plans in place for identified talent
- percentage of identified talent promoted to next level
- program feedback.

B. Manager Development

Manager development is one of the most talked about topics in people management. It is another area where organizations waste vast amounts of time and money, often with little or no result. It has become overly complex and an industry in itself, when really it should be very simple.

The first step for manager development is to clarify the role, accountabilities, authorities and expectations of managers. It is only after the role of a manager in an organization is clearly defined that the required knowledge, skills and behaviors can then be accurately defined. This critical step is missed by many organizations.

In The Leadership Framework, the role of a manager is to *achieve the business goals set for them and, at the same time, provide an environment that allows their team to be effective and satisfied with their work while developing their full potential.* Therefore, managerial work falls into two broad components:

- **The technical work** such as delivering the core components of the role, completing the assigned tasks as part of the business plan and developing new methods.
- **The enabling work** that supports and sustains the delivery of the technical work. This enabling work consists of:
  - ➤ **The programming work** which includes planning and scheduling work, preparing budgets, monitoring progress and reporting.
  - ➤ **The people work** which includes building productive working relationships across the organization, managing team performance and integrating the work of the team.

As managers need the skills for all aspects of their role, development activities for managers must be focused on the ability to deliver outputs and the ability to perform the enabling work.

Typically, 'technical' aspects of development are handled through recruitment of people with the required technical skills, such as accountants or electricians, with ongoing professional development provided through professional associations or tertiary institutes. The focus of this book is on the 'people' aspects of managerial leadership. Furthermore, as The Leadership Framework provides an integrated system of people management, together with the related programming work for people managers at all levels, it can be used as the basis for the training and development for all people leaders (see the following diagram).

The Leadership Framework

i. Skill requirements for every manager at every level.

At the manager level, the knowledge and skills required are specified in Leading Yourself and Leading People of The Leadership Framework. To be successful, managers need to demonstrate competency in four areas:

a. Understand your role as a manager.
   - Understand the role of the manager, including manager accountabilities and authorities.
   - Understand and respect the role of others, including the role of team members, peers, their own manager, specialists and corporate functions.

b. Build and lead an effective team.

To be successful, managers must build and lead an effective team so that each member is fully committed to and capable of moving in the direction set. To achieve this outcome requires a strong manager-team member working relationship based on systemic trust and fairness. To achieve this outcome, managers must be able to:

- Provide a safe work environment.
- Create effective roles and put good people in them.
- Effectively assign and assess work.
- Develop team capability.
- Recognize and reward good work.
- Build great teamwork.

c. Continuously improve and manage change.
In addition to the execution of the day-to-day operational work, managers identify ways for work to be done more effectively and efficiently. Therefore, they must be able to:

- Continuously improve the work of their team.
- Manage change within their team.

d. Build constructive working relationships.
The work environment critically influences an individual's ability to do their best work. The use of good interpersonal skills (by everybody) will assist in establishing more constructive behaviors and provide some 'social glue' – especially in managing conflict. However, interpersonal skills have limited value in a workplace and/or a working relationship which is otherwise flawed in its design or is subject to ineffective leadership.

Building constructive working relationships is about:

- Ensuring the working organization in their area of accountability supports constructive work.
- Understanding and respecting the role of others.
- Establish values and standards of behavior.
- Applying conflict management tools and skills to appropriately engage and openly resolve issues that may otherwise impede effective working.

ii. Skill requirements for managers of managers.

To be successful, managers of managers need to demonstrate competency as a manager (above) plus competency in the additional knowledge and skill requirements for executive leaders. At the manager of managers' level, these additional skill requirements are developed from the 'Leading the organization' section of The Leadership Framework.

a. Business and organizational leadership.
Managers of managers are accountable to lead the organization to achieve its business purpose. This requires managers of managers to provide the appropriate systems of work (structures, policies, procedures and communication and information technologies) to enable employees to perform to their full capability and to shape a productive workplace culture. They do this by having the skills to create and deliver systems of work to:

- Implement business strategy.
- Design the organization.
- Design and maintain productive systems of work.
- Enable systemic trust and fairness.
- Build workforce capability.
- Manage strategic relationships.

b. As a manager once removed.

Managers of managers have a large impact on the work environment of their business unit. They are not only accountable for the output of a team of teams, they also have a specific working relationship as the manager once removed (MOR) with the team members of their direct reporting managers. As the MOR, they provide the foundation for systemic trust and fairness throughout the organization.

The MOR must be able to:

- Ensure the consistency and quality of leadership to their employees once removed.
- Ensure fair treatment and justice.
- Develop capability for the future.
- Integrate work across teams/departments/ divisions/ the whole organization.

iii. Monitoring and review.

Manager development programs need to be continually monitored and reviewed. Individual assessments can be made as part of the organization's ongoing performance review process. Other methods include:

- Specific skills assessments.
- Employee survey results such as employee engagement surveys.

C. Skills/competency programs

Skills programs are designed to ensure that tasks are performed in accordance with required specifications. They define the specific knowledge and skill requirements for a specific task or for a role made up of a number of tasks. They may or may not be linked to a formal competency program, such as those defined by a vocational, educational or training authority.

Organizations use skills programs for many reasons. The main reasons are:

- As a tool to identify and close gaps in knowledge or skills.
- To comply with industrial, legal or regulatory requirements.
- Career development.
- As a tool to drive behaviors and values.
- As a tool to align people to the organization's objectives.
- To provide greater clarity for people on their role expectations.
- As part of a structured framework to evaluate and reward staff.

Skills programs are important for areas where:

- The performance requirement for a task/role (e.g. forklift operation) needs to be exact for compliance reasons (legal, regulatory or organizational requirement).
- An injury or illness may occur if the role or task is not performed in a prescribed manner.
- Standards of performance need to be clearly specified, and this cannot be done in any other manner.
- They provide a competitive advantage.

i. Issues.

Skills programs are suited for roles required to perform specific tasks which are relatively consistent over time. They do, however, have some issues. They can:

- Have too many competencies for roles, some of which are not relevant or partially relevant.
- Overly prescribe each competency.
- Become overly complex and time consuming with implementation, maintenance, tracking and continuous improvement requirements.

- Have time-consuming review and assessment processes.
- Have automatic pay progression resulting in many staff being paid at the highest level without the requirement to use the skills.
- Unclear or no career development outcomes.

ii. Considerations for the design of skills programs.
Each organization should develop its own criteria for a skills program. When considering the design of a skills program, points to consider are:

- Skills programs need to be designed to meet specific outcomes. The more outcomes required, the more complex the skills program becomes and the more administration is required.
- Just because a role has some tasks that require specific skills or a competency does not mean that a program must be developed for the whole role. A program can be developed just for one task or a portion of a role.
- Skills programs are designed to ensure that the job is done in accordance with a specification. They do not always need to deliver formal qualifications or to align to national/state standards.
- Skills programs are best suited where employees are required to perform specific tasks that are relatively consistent over time. This is typically characterized by Stratum I roles (i.e. frontline roles). The work of these roles is mostly stable, characterized by tasks that typically remain the same over time, and the annual goals assigned as part of the performance planning process effectively remain the same from year to year.

iii. Monitoring and review.
Skills/competency programs usually have a skills assessment process built into the design of the program.

Key Concepts

- The aim of employee development is to ensure all employees have the knowledge, skills, experience and behaviors required to perform their role effectively.
- Three of the key workforce development initiatives are:
  - ➤ Talent identification and development.
  - ➤ Manager development.
  - ➤ Skills/competency programs.
- The aims of talent development programs are to:
  - ➤ Accurately identify talented individuals.
  - ➤ Improve the retention and performance of talented individuals.
  - ➤ Build a pipeline of capable individuals who can move into key roles.
  - ➤ Actively engage all of the organization in talent identification and development.
- In The Leadership Framework, the manager once removed (MOR) is accountable for developing capability to meet future business needs, and therefore, for talent pool development.
- The first step for manager development is to clarify the role, accountabilities, authorities and expectations of managers in the organization. It is only after the role of a manager in an organization is clearly defined that the required knowledge, skills, experience and behaviors can then be accurately defined.
- In The Leadership Framework, the role of a manager is to *achieve the business goals set for them and, at*

the same time, provide an environment that allows their team to be effective and satisfied with their work while developing their full potential.

- Skills programs are designed to ensure that tasks are performed in accordance with required specifications. They define the specific knowledge and skill requirements for a specific task or for a role made up of a number of tasks. They may or may not be linked to a formal competency program, such as those defined by a vocational, educational or training authority.
- Skills programs are important for areas where:
  - ➤ The performance requirement for a task/role (e.g. forklift operation) needs to be exact for compliance reasons (legal, regulatory or organizational requirement).
  - ➤ An injury or illness may occur if the role or task is not performed in a prescribed manner.
  - ➤ Standards of performance need to be clearly specified, and this cannot be done in any other manner.
  - ➤ They provide a competitive advantage.

Tips for Getting Started

1. Review your talent management process. How are talented employees identified? What is the role of the manager once removed?
2. In manager development, do you use a framework to identify what managers must be, know and do? How does this compare to The Leadership Framework?

Additional information available at www.theleadershipframework.com.au

- Model for individual capability.
- Determining performance improvement actions.
- Accountability for employee development.
- Ways to develop your team.
- Tools and resources – Development plan template.
- Tools and resources – Development plan example.
- Talent identification and development.
- Tools and resources – Retention risk assessment.
- Creating a skills program.
- Tools and resources – Career conversations guide for employees.
- Tools and resources – Career conversations guide for the manager once removed.
- Tools and resources – Example - Organizational skills program document - design principles, accountabilities and authorities.

Chapter 8

How to remove employees

From time to time all organizations need to remove employees. This needs to be done in a fair and respectful manner while at the same time supporting those who remain.

PART OF BUILDING WORKFORCE CAPABILITY is the ability to remove excess or unwanted employees. Systemic non-management of individual performance, the non-management of the total number of employees or a significant change in the economic environment will impact overall workforce capability. Therefore, all organizations need effective systems of work to fairly assess and possibly remove people who do not fit the organization's needs. This means having effective performance management and fair treatment systems for the management of individuals and having effective workforce management systems for organizational change.

Common removal strategies

Two of the key initiatives of an employee management strategy are:

- Improving the management of individual performance effectiveness.
- Improving redundancy and redeployment processes.

A. Improving individual performance effectiveness

Managing performance is essential to the efficient functioning of any organization. Underperformance occurs when the activities and/or output of a team member are below what is required. Underperformance of itself is not normally the major issue. It is the failure or inability to correct the underperformance that causes long-term issues. If left uncorrected, it can affect the whole business unit.

i. Process to improve individual performance effectiveness.
   a. Establish reasons for underperformance.
      The first step is to identify the reason or reasons for underperformance. To do this, the manager must initiate a discussion with the team member. While there is a tendency to focus on the individual and to try and 'fix' the person, remember that underperformance may be caused by one factor or multiple factors as individual capability is impacted by the working organization (i.e. the individual capability of the person's manager and the organization's structure, role relationships and systems of work; see Chapter 4 "How to improve the working organization"). Therefore, the impact of these areas on a team member's performance effectiveness should be the initial focus. The meeting should be non-confrontational or non-threatening in nature.

In the meeting, the manager must be able to present objective evidence to support their assertion of underperformance, such as specific instances of poor behavior. The aim is to get the individual's view on why things are not working.

It is important to note that some causes may not only be outside the individual's control but also outside the organization's control, for example, family problems. This section does not cover personal issues as they can be varied in nature. In such circumstances, managers should seek advice from a human resources professional, or they may need to refer to a third party for assistance. In such circumstances, the person may need more flexibility or time from the manager.

b. Develop appropriate actions.
Once issues are identified, the manager must take corrective action. Common issues are:

- **Unsupportive organizational structure, role design or systems of work.**
It is the manager's accountability to provide a working environment that supports productive work. Therefore, if performance issues are caused by:
    - unclear accountabilities, authorities or role relationships, or
    - the position description is no longer relevant to the position, or
    - a poorly designed role, or
    - a vague performance development plan, or
    - where systems of work do not support the work,

then it is the accountability of the manager to identify these issues and to promptly correct this situation.

- **Poor understanding of role and accountabilities.**

If the cause of the underperformance is a lack of clarity or understanding of what is expected, the line manager should immediately correct this by restating the expectations verbally and perhaps in writing.

The manager needs to ensure the team member is clear on the requirements of the role. For each task the manager must reset:

- The **C**ontext of the task.
- The **P**urpose of the task.
- The **Q**uantity of output required.
- The **Q**uality of output required.
- The **R**esources available to do the work.
- The **T**iming of the above output requirements.

Simply restating and clarifying the work requirements is often enough to put the team member back on track.

However, managers must also ensure all team members can answer the following questions:

- Where are we heading (as a team)?
- What is my role?
- How is my performance measured?

This will provide further clarity of requirements.

- **Lack of skills or knowledge.**

The manager needs to assess the gap between current competency and the competency required to improve performance. Sometimes professional assessment may be required. If so, the method of assessment should be discussed with Human Resources.

Once the skill gap is identified, the manager should arrange corrective action. This may be as simple as 'on the job instruction' or may require other development strategies. See Chapter 7 "How to develop workforce capability".

- **Fitness to do the job.**

If a team member is deemed not 'fit' to do their job, either physically or psychologically, by their manager or by their own admission, a professional assessment is usually required to establish the cause.

Key factors to determine will be:

- Whether the restriction is permanent.
- If not, how long the incapacity will last.
- What temporary duties can be safely given.

Where a team member completes a fitness/medical assessment and it is assessed they are 'unfit' to perform any work, they can usually be moved to a more suitable role or dismissed from the organization. In this process, managers need to strictly adhere to organizational policies and procedures and any agreements or legislation that covers employees in the area.

- **Demonstration of unwanted behaviors.**

Unacceptable behavior, not immediately corrected, becomes behavior that is acceptable not just for the individual but for the whole team. To correct this, the manager must give the team member specific examples of the unacceptable behavior and advise them of the consequences if the behavior continues. If they do continue the unwanted behaviors, the manager must initiate removal.

Non-specific generalizations will not remediate the poor behavior and may even make the situation worse.

- **Excessive absence.**

Specific evidence of the pattern of leave and the history of excessive leave or absenteeism must be presented to and discussed with the team member. To assist in the determination of the issues and actions, managers should refer to the organization's sick leave policy/procedure and consult with human resources.

It is important to remember that:

- If an employee is genuinely sick, they may have entitlements under the organization's sick leave policy or legislation.
- If absences are long term, then refer to actions in 'Fitness to do the job', above, for the appropriate action.

ii. Accountabilities

Position	Accountability
Team member	i. To participate in the discussion to identify the cause of underperformance, openly and honestly. ii. To cooperate with the development and implementation of plans/strategies to correct the underperformance. iii. To seek professional assistance if required to manage health issues or lack of competency.
Manager	i. To initiate, arrange and conduct a meeting to discuss performance. ii. To identify issues affecting performance effectiveness. iii. To take action and allow time for the team member to correct performance. iv. To monitor the performance of the team member and give feedback as required. v. To discuss team member's performance with the manager once removed where assistance is required, alternative views are needed or the outcome may result in a request to remove the team member.

Manager once removed	i. Ensure consistency and quality of leadership for their team member once removed by: <ul><li>Coaching their direct report managers on their leadership effectiveness.</li><li>Shaping the workplace culture and setting expectations of behavior for all managers in the business unit.</li><li>Reviewing managerial decisions of their direct reports as part of performance assessment.</li></ul> ii. Ensure fair treatment by: <ul><li>Providing objectivity for decisions affecting their team members once removed.</li><li>Ensuring consistent application of policies across the business unit.</li><li>Deciding on promotion/demotion/dismissal of team members once removed.</li><li>Deciding appeal outcomes.</li></ul> iii. Integrate the work of their team of teams by: <ul><li>Setting the context for work of the business unit.</li><li>Establishing systems of work that integrate the end-to-end processes of the business unit and align work across teams.</li><li>Ensuring their managers collaborate constructively to achieve the overall plan of the business unit.</li></ul>
Divisional HR manager	i. To provide advice and support and to coach line managers as requested or required. ii. To provide advice and support to employees when required.

B. Improving organizational redundancy and redeployment processes

Redundancy occurs where a job performed by an employee ceases to exist so the person is retrenched or redeployed. It is often the result of:

- Improvements in technology.
- Globalization.
- Changes to the direction of a business.
- Changes in demand for the organization's products/ services.
- Managers not planning their people resources effectively.

It often occurs:

- In difficult economic times where organizations are forced to conduct layoffs to ensure long-term survival.
- To improve profit margins.

Furthermore, companies or departments that are retrenching employees are often changing their mix of skills at the same time, so retrenchments and hiring occur simultaneously. Whether being performed as a necessity for survival, to improve profit or to make the organization more competitive, there are several misconceptions about the impacts and outcomes of restructuring. These misconceptions include:

- *Cutting employees automatically boosts profits*. Profitability does not necessarily follow retrenchments as organizations underestimate the costs of restructure and its short- and long-term impacts on those who remain. Profitability sometimes drops.
- *Cutting employee numbers boosts productivity*. Research shows that productivity levels following retrenchment are mixed. In most instances, in the short-

term, downsizing detrimentally impacts the quality of products and services and does not necessarily lead to improvements in quality in the long term. For the majority of remaining employees, including managers, downsizing does have an adverse effect on their workload, morale and commitment.

- *Reducing employees always results in reduced costs.* There are significant direct and indirect costs in downsizing. Direct costs include:
  - ➢ Redundancy pay.
  - ➢ Payment in lieu of notice.
  - ➢ Accrued annual and long-service leave.
  - ➢ Administrative costs.
  - ➢ Outplacement expenses.
  - ➢ Cost of rehiring.
  - ➢ Potential ongoing legal expenses.
  - ➢ Increased training costs for new employees or those who remain but are in new roles.

There are also indirect costs. These include:
- ➢ Low morale.
- ➢ Risk-averse survivors.
- ➢ Reduced productivity.
- ➢ Eroded career structures.
- ➢ Increased employee turnover.
- ➢ Loss of institutional memory.
- ➢ Potential loss of business.
- ➢ Loss of trust in management.
- ➢ Decreased levels of customer service.
- ➢ Loss of external contacts and business relationships.
- ➢ Increased security costs.

Moreover, there are community costs which include:
- ➢ Increased social security costs e.g. unemployment benefits.
- ➢ Increased taxes.

> Stress on families.
> Stress on small communities.

i. Alternatives to redundancy.

Due to the significant impact of layoffs on people and the organization, it makes sense, as a first step, to spend time and effort on studying how to reduce the need to lay off employees or at least to minimize the impact of such actions. Depending on the reasons for the change, there are a number of actions that can be taken.

a) Reduce the need for redundancy.
   - Cut other expenses.
   - Find ways to increase revenue.
   - Freeze hiring.
   - Cross train/multiskill employees.
   - Eliminate or reduce the use of casuals, agency staff or contractors.
   - Improve workforce planning processes.
   - Reduce or eliminate overtime.
   - Consult employees on expense reduction/ productivity improvement.
   - Adjust compensation.
     > Freeze salaries.
     > Bonus/incentive reductions or elimination.
     > Salary reductions.
     > Trade pay cuts for equity in the organization.
     > Adjust benefits.

b) Reschedule work hours.
   - Voluntary days off without pay.
   - Ensure employees take unused annual and long-service leave.
   - Unpaid sabbaticals and/or secondments to other organizations.
   - Eliminate overtime.

- Reduce work hours.
- Sponsor full-time tertiary studies.

c) Restructure the workforce.
- Job sharing.
- Relocate employees.
- Retrain current employees.
- Natural attrition.
- Internal deployment.
- External deployment.

d) Consider other strategies.
- Enable employee buyout.
- Create a temporary employee pool to use as casuals and for special projects.
- Offer voluntary early retirement.
- Maintain a rigorous performance review process.
- Consult employees – invite their input.
- Use natural attrition over time.

ii. Handling involuntary terminations.

Communicating news of the termination of their employment to those who must leave an organization is always difficult. In conducting involuntary termination meetings, it's important to anticipate a variety of reactions ranging from fear, anger and frustration to the feeling of rejection. These are normal reactions to the news of losing a job, but managers should prepare appropriate responses.

Attempt to manage the situation in a positive, forward-thinking manner through sensitivity, support and encouragement. Do not try and 'soften the blow' by allowing the laid-off employee to think there is any chance of reversing the decision. For example, do not say, "If it were my decision alone, I wouldn't do this." The message that needs to be delivered is that this is a final decision and the employee can apply for other posted positions. However, the decision for today's action is final.

In preparing for, conducting and following up on this meeting, remember that the objectives are to:

- Communicate the decision in a clear, consistent and professional manner.
- Present the decision as irrevocable.
- Demonstrate honesty, integrity and respect.
- Maintain confidentiality.
- Describe outplacement support and encourage the employee to participate.
- Allow the employee to react.
- Offer support and compassion.
- Encourage the employee to take positive actions.

It is important that the employees who have been selected for layoff understand the basis for the layoff. The rationale for the layoff and the consistency and truthfulness of the message that is communicated is important from a legal and emotional standpoint.

Important points to remember:

- Don't begin with small talk.
- Don't debate.
- Don't forget that the employee will forget much of what you say.
- Don't give personal, financial or legal advice.
- If you don't know the answer to a question, say you'll get back to them.
- Don't make promises that you may not be able to keep.
- This is not the time for a performance appraisal.
- Don't be defensive or feel you must persuade the person the action is justified.
- However difficult the meeting is for you, it is tougher for him or her.

- Grievances and accusations from the past are truly history.
- Do not criticize the organization.
- Don't argue about anything.
- It isn't helpful to say, "I know how you feel."
- Do not discuss your personal relationship with the employee. Arrange to talk about the 'good old days' another time.
- Own the message. Don't say it wasn't your decision or that the decision was someone else's.

iii. Communicate to remaining employees.

A reduction in workforce can also be traumatic for those who stay. After a layoff, remaining employees are often less engaged and, as a result, are less productive so it's important for managers to consider, in advance, what they will tell their remaining employees.

As those who remain may take on some of the work from their departed colleagues, it is important for managers to communicate how the layoffs will impact the day-to-day work and provide support to prevent burnout. Alternatively, there may be some relief as some employees may have already seen the change coming and are relieved that it is over. Either way, managers should take the following steps to support those who remain:

- Explain the direction of the business and the specific actions that the organization's leadership is taking to avoid future business challenges.
- Work with human resources to understand how this conversation may differ for particular individuals or workforce segments (e.g. those who worked more closely with those who were laid off may react differently).

- Explain to employees what has happened and why (focus on the business rationale).
- Explain that departing colleagues will be taken care of (provide generalities of severance benefits but do not provide details of packages).
- Do not discuss specifics about individual employees.
- Announce that layoffs are complete as soon as possible. Be careful in the wording of the announcement to avoid setting expectations in the event that additional layoffs are being planned/ considered.
- Give employees a chance to express their feelings and ask questions. The types of emotions you can expect include anger, guilt and stress.
- Remain visible and available to the remaining employees. Communicate an open-door policy for any questions and concerns.
- Talk about any issues regarding changes to the day-to-day work of employees and the department.

While most employees are less likely to leave the organization after a layoff has occurred due to fewer labor market opportunities, high potentials are more likely to leave than the general population. This may leave the organization at risk of losing some of its most valuable employees.

iv. Accountabilities.
Manager's role:
- Ensure HR's involvement from the outset. The earlier HR is involved in the planning process, the more likely is a successful outcome.
- Examine the alternatives to retrenchment.
- Determine, with the human resources, the criteria for selecting those to be retrenched.
- Determine the roles to be removed.

- Communicate and implement changes in the team.

HR's role:
- Review legal obligations.
- Determine, with the manager, the criteria for selecting those to be retrenched.
- Determine the length of notice to be given.
- Provide advice on communicating the redundancies.
- Approve severance packages.
- Train and support managers in implementing the workforce reduction.
- Organize outplacement services.
- Recommend a plan for managing the those who remain.

Key Concepts

- Part of building workforce capability is the ability to remove unneeded or unwanted employees. Systemic non-management of individual performance, the non-management of the total number of employees or a significant change in the economic environment will impact overall workforce capability.
- All organizations need effective systems of work to fairly assess and possibly remove people who do not fit the organization's needs.
- Two of the key initiatives of an employee management strategy are:
  - ➤ improving the management of individual performance effectiveness
  - ➤ improving redundancy and redeployment processes.

- Common reasons for underperformance are:
  - ➢ Unsupportive organizational structure, poor role design or systems of work.
  - ➢ Poor understanding of role and accountabilities.
  - ➢ Lack of skills or knowledge.
  - ➢ Excessive absence.
  - ➢ Fitness to do the job.
  - ➢ Demonstration of unwanted behaviors.
- There are several misconceptions about the impacts and outcomes of restructuring. These include:
  - ➢ Reducing employees always results in reduced costs. There are significant direct and indirect costs in downsizing, including community costs.
  - ➢ Cutting employees automatically boosts profits. Profitability does not necessarily follow retrenchments as organizations underestimate the costs of restructuring and its short- and long-term impacts on those who remain.
  - ➢ Cutting employee numbers boosts productivity. Research shows that productivity levels following retrenchment are mixed. In most instances, in the short term, downsizing detrimentally impacts the quality of products and services and does not necessarily lead to improvements in quality in the long term.
- For the majority of those who remain, including managers, downsizing does have an adverse effect on their workload, morale and commitment.
- Due to the significant impact of layoffs on people and the organization, it makes sense, as a first step, to spend time and effort on studying how to reduce the need to lay off employees or at least to minimize the impact of such actions.
- Communicating to those who must leave an organization is always difficult. In conducting involuntary termination meetings, it's important to anticipate a

variety of reactions ranging from fear, anger and frustration to the feeling of rejection.

- A reduction in the workforce can be very traumatic for those who stay. After a layoff, remaining employees are often less engaged and, as a result, are less productive so it's important to consider, in advance, what you will tell your remaining employees.
- While most employees are less likely to leave the organization after a layoff due to fewer labor market opportunities, high potentials are more likely to leave than the general population. This leaves organizations at risk of losing some of their most valuable employees.

Tips for Getting Started

1. Review your manager training. Do managers have the knowledge and skills to assess the impacts on employee effectiveness? Do they look at the whole working environment or just try to fix the person?

2. If you are planning to lay off employees, hold a meeting with senior leaders. Outline the true direct and indirect costs of the layoff and assess the true costs. Look for alternatives.

3. Assess how your process for redundancy supports those who stay.

4. To gain a better understanding of the impact of the working organization on each employee's personal effectiveness, read the second book in the Leadership Framework Series titled, *Don't Fix Me, Fix the Workplace: A Guide to Building Constructive Working Relationships* by Peter Mills.

5. To gain a better understanding of the managing change and continuous improvement, read the first book in the Leadership Framework Series titled, *Leading People – The 10 Things Successful Managers Know and Do* by Peter Mills.

Additional information available at www.theleadershipframework.com.au

- What is work?
- How to effectively assign a task.
- Assessing individual performance effectiveness.
- Principles for organizational design.
- Designing effective roles.
- Principles for design of a system of work.
- Process for designing/reviewing systems of work.
- Tools and resources – Systems of work effectiveness scan.
- Resourcing options.
- Barriers to continuous improvement.
- Enabling continuous improvement.
- Leading change.
- Understanding resistance to change.
- Tools and resources - Leading change checklist.
- Tools and resources - Change management action plan template.
- Tools and resources - Change management communication plan template.
- Tools and resources - Change management systems of work plan template.
- Tools and resources - Change management training plan template.
- Tools and resources - Change management people resourcing plan template.

Chapter 9

Cultural change

In order to change an organization's culture, real and significant adjustments must be made to the whole working organization.

IN CHAPTERS 5 TO 8, the initiatives to improve workplace capability were focused on specific issues such as attraction, retention, development or removal. As such, they required changes focused on specific parts of the organization. Some interventions, however, are more complex and require the integration of many actions to achieve the required outcome. One of these is changing organizational culture.

Culture is the shared assumptions and beliefs a group of people have about certain behaviors based on what that group values or does not value. The more beliefs people share, the stronger the culture. Culture gives people a framework within which they can begin to organize their world and their behavior.

To change culture requires changes to the working organization so that the right working environment is created that both enables and sustains the desired culture. This means reviewing and possibly changing:

- Managerial leadership practices/behavior.
- The organization's systems and structure.
- The symbols created in relation to the above, such as recognition, uniforms, car parking spaces and rewards.

These impacts on employee behavior are shown in the diagram below:

Impacts on employee behaviour

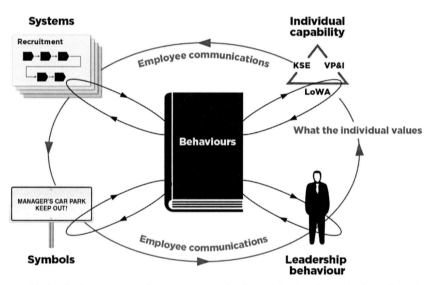

Note: In the above diagram organizational design is part of 'Systems'.

The process to implement a new workplace culture is no different than the process to implement any workplace strategy outlined in Chapter 3 "Planning, monitoring and reporting for workplace capability". In the examples below, however, some steps have been further dissected for clarity, while others have been combined for brevity.

Common strategies to change culture

While there is often talk about changing organizational culture, the difficult question is, "What culture do you want to have?" Unless the answer to this question is clearly defined, the organization may not achieve the required change or the newly created culture may not be what was planned.

Two common types of cultural change attempted by organizations are:

- A constructive working culture.
- A culture where safety is a priority.

The following examples illustrate the method to change an organizational culture. The actual actions required will vary from organization to organization.

A. Example of the process to implement a constructive working culture

i. Define the culture.
   In this example I have used The Leadership Framework's definition of constructive working culture: *To create a place where people work together in a positive manner, doing productive work to achieve organizational objectives.*

ii. Broadly outline the actions required to achieve the change.
   When looking to create a constructive culture, the typical response is to focus on interpersonal skills. On the face of it, this makes sense as the use of good interpersonal skills (by everybody) assists in establishing more constructive behaviors and provides some 'social glue'. However, this is only a band-aid solution as good interpersonal skills have limited value in a workplace which is otherwise flawed in its design or subject to ineffective leadership.

To build constructive working relationships that enables productive work requires senior leaders to review the operation of the whole working organization. The basis for collaboration must be built into the organization's structure, roles and the organization's systems of work, all of which are activated by effective managerial leadership.

The Leadership Framework model for constructive working relationships will be used. The required actions are shown in the diagram below.

Model for constructive working relationships

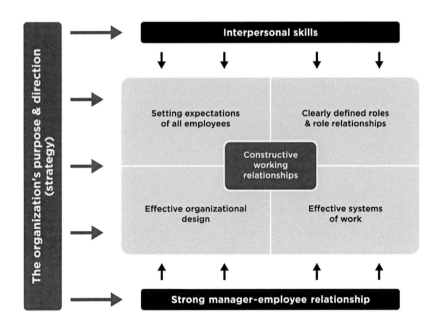

iii. Define the requirements and actions.

The Leadership Framework model has six independent but interrelated parts. The context for each part of the model is defined by the organization's purpose and direction (strategy). These six parts are:

a) Setting Expectations of All Employees.

The first step in building constructive working relationships is to set expectations on how people are to work together. This includes ensuring behaviors such as honesty, integrity, respect for others and collaboration are embedded in these expectations so they become the social norms for the organization.

To work together in a constructive manner requires all employees to:

- Fulfill commitments made
- Bring their full capability to work
- Continue to develop their performance effectiveness
- Provide their manager with feedback
- Work together productively.

These 'expectations of all employees' are expanded in the table in Chapter 6 "How to retain talent". The delivery of these expectations will reduce the causes of conflict and enable people to work together constructively.

Actions
- Communicate new expectations to all employees.
- Integrate the new behaviors into the performance management system and the recognition and reward systems.

b) Effective Organizational Design.

An organization's design provides the shared understanding of accountability and authority that exists between people whose work is aligned and integrated to deliver the organization's purpose and direction. Unless this work is properly aligned, with clear handoff points for work, silos will develop and workarounds will occur. Issues of accountability and authority may occur, causing functions to start duplicating the work of other divisions to achieve outcomes. Alternatively, employees will try to resolve issues by developing personal relationships across functional boundaries. They will start swapping favors to get work done. New employees, who have not had time to establish long-term relationships, will get frustrated as they try to deliver their work. Clearly, this is not acceptable.

Getting structure wrong can create an environment that results in negative behaviors such as:

- Undermining
- Micromanaging
- Workarounds
- Empire building
- Job protection

Such behavior results in a loss of trust in the organization, a loss of confidence in the system of management and frustration around the ability to get work done. It impacts the ability of people to work together.

Actions

- Review and clarify 'handoff' point accountabilities and authorities between core functions such as sales vs marketing and manufacturing vs service.
- Review and clarify the accountabilities and authorities of corporate functions such as human resources and finance. Assess how they align with the accountabilities and authorities of core divisions and the line managers in those divisions (see Typical Accountabilities and Authorities for Corporate Human Resources Functions in Chapter 4 "How to improve the working organization").

c) Clearly Defined Roles and Role Relationships.
While aligning each function in the organization is essential to enable constructive working relationships, so too is the alignment of roles. This is especially important for specialist roles. Specialist roles, such as technical specialists and planners, exist to support managerial work. They are critical to the effectiveness of the working organization as these roles support the line by providing expertise or specialist services.

Typical issues for employees working with specialists are:
- What is the role of the specialist?
- What are the specialist's accountabilities and authorities?
- How do they integrate with manager accountabilities and authorities?
- How do they impact team members' account-abilities and authorities?
- How do they work with other team members?

Actions
- Audit specialist roles within teams to ensure their accountabilities and authorities are clear and in alignment and do not conflict with the line manager's role or that of other team members. For example, is the role of the specialist to monitor the work of the team or coordinate the work of the team? Do they advise team members on new methods or can they change methods?

d) Effective Systems of Work.
Systems of work, such as policies and processes, enable people to work together so their design is essential to enable constructive working relationships.

Systems of work:
- Facilitate work across functions, across teams and within teams.
- Provide the standardizing methods and boundaries for work.
- Align people and work with legislation, social norms and the organization's values.
- Allow the leadership team to monitor and verify that the organization's purpose and strategy are being achieved in accordance with its cultural, ethical and moral standards.
- Create customs, practices, traditions, beliefs and assumptions, which in turn help create the organization's culture.

Actions
- Perform a "systems scan". Ensure all systems of work conform to The Leadership Framework's design principles. As a minimum, all systems of work must:
  - Have a designated system owner.
  - Be designed to meet the needs of the customer/end user/beneficiary of the system.
  - Be consistent with legislation, regulations and other corporate policies and standards.
  - Specify working relationships in the system of work.
  - Engage all stakeholders on the development and use of the system.
  - Equalize the treatment of employees unless there is a business reason not to equalize.
  - Have a continuous improvement process built into the system design.

See Chapter 4 – "How to improve the working organization".

e) Strong Manager-Employee Relationship.
The foundation of constructive working relationships is the manager-employee working relationship. A strong manager-employee working relationship can only be achieved where managers have strong personal authority earned through effective performance in their role. See Chapter 4 "How to improve the working organization".

Actions

- Train managers in principles and practices of The Leadership Framework. See skill requirements for managers in Chapter 7 "How to improve workforce capability".

f) Interpersonal Skills.
As people are social beings and work is an environment where social interaction is required to achieve business outcomes, managers need skills for dealing with people management issues. These skills must be focused on getting work done in a constructive and productive manner.

Actions

- Train managers how to handle specific manager-team member interactions, that is, how to:
  - ➢ Address conflict.
  - ➢ Address unacceptable performance.
  - ➢ Take corrective action.
  - ➢ Handle complaints.
  - ➢ Manage change.
  - ➢ Recognize good work.

iv. Complete the planning process.
For each action create measures and targets, define accountability for implementation, cascade the strategy and implement monitoring and reporting processes. Use the monitoring and reporting mechanisms to define future work requirements.

B. Example of the process to create a culture where safety is a priority

i. Define the culture.

Every organization is different in terms of its health and safety risks. Therefore, each organization needs its own unique health and safety strategy. Some organizations take a broad brush approach by training all employees on the importance of safety and state that 'Safety is everyone's responsibility,' but this is not really effective for the following reasons:

- Risks vary considerably both across organizations and within organizations.
- The level of knowledge, skills and experience required by people and organizations varies significantly.
- Accountability for health and safety is different for different functions and levels within an organization.

In this example, a 'safety culture' is defined as a place where all people:

- 'Actively care' about their own safety and the safety of others.
- Feel accountable for safe work practices and pursue them on a daily basis.
- Identify unsafe conditions and behaviors and intervene to correct them.
- See safety as the number one priority of the organization (ahead of efficiency and productivity).

ii. Broadly outline the actions required to achieve the change.

A new safety strategy will be implemented based on three foundations:

- Effective leadership.
- Clear accountabilities and authorities.
- An easy to use safety management system.

This will be enabled by having:

- Employees trained to competently perform their tasks.
- Effective consultation and communication.
- Hazard identification and risk control.
- Effective measurement, monitoring, reporting and review processes.

The framework is shown in the diagram below.

Safety improvement strategy

iii. Define the requirements and actions.

To achieve zero injuries, seven independent but interrelated actions will be taken.

a) Effective leadership.

The organization's senior leaders must provide the leadership and direction for other managers to perform their role effectively. This means delivering the safety mission, strategy, objectives and targets and providing managers with the systems and skills to perform their role.

Safety must be part of a manager's day-to-day work requirements and not a separate activity or accountability. All managers must be held to account for delivery of safe working practices.

Actions
- Integrate safety strategy into divisional strategic workforce plans.
- Provide visible leadership.
- Engage the workforce in safety improvement.
- Strengthen the manager/employee/contractor working relationship in relation to safety.

b) Clear accountabilities and authorities.
All employees need to be clear on their safety accountabilities.

Actions
- Create a safety organization structure designed to deliver new strategy, with clear accountabilities and authorities for each role or group of roles.
- Define the specific accountabilities and authorities for the following groups:
  - Board of directors
  - Safety committees
  - Key risk steering committees
  - Manager roles (and ensure the right work is done at the right level of management)
  - All employees
  - Corporate safety teams

c) Hazard identification and risk control.
A focused program will be developed to understand key risks (i.e. high risk areas and high frequency incidents).

Actions
- Define an owner for each site – no shared accountability.
- Identify risks.
- Create action to control key risks.
- Develop an audit process.

d) Easy to use safety management system.
Complex systems and lack of knowledge regarding how to use the systems create difficulty for managers who have to manage safety. This is particularly true for most managers who may only have an incident once or twice a year. Even if they want to do the right thing, they do not know what to do and do not know how to get help so systems are not followed. To engage managers in safety, the systems and processes must be easy to use.

Actions
- Streamline and simplify safety systems.
- Simplify reporting.
- All systems of work in the safety management system must follow the eight design principles of The Leadership Framework. See Chapter 4 "How to improve the working organization".

e) Competency training.
Competency training is integral to any risk management process. This is increasingly so as many previously required inspection processes have been or are in the process of being transferred from regulators to licensed third parties.

Actions
- Improve safety induction for new team members.
- All managers must ensure their team members have the safety competencies for the work they are performing.

f) Consultation and communication.
Health and safety communication should commence at the pre-employment stage and continue as part of the day-to-day work.

Actions
- Ensure operators and managers are consulted in the development of safe working procedures.
- Clearly communicate the organization's strategy to improve safety performance and progress.
- Provide clear and relevant messaging to all employees.
- Commence safety messaging at the pre-employment stage.

g) Measure, monitor, report and review.
Currently the organization focuses on lost time injuries (LTIs). This is inadequate as it does not monitor if other organizational and legislative requirements are being satisfied. Although an important measure, the focus on LTIs is an outcome indicator that reflects past actions only. It does not give managers an understanding of what is being done now to improve safety. If managers do not know what is being done now, then they cannot demonstrate due diligence.

Furthermore, focusing only on failure and not on the positive things being done to improve safety performance has created a culture where having an injury at work is seen as something extremely bad. There is more concern with the impact of the LTI on manager reputation and performance than on the injured person. Some managers 'hide' LTIs because they dread being put through the third degree and perhaps having their remuneration impacted.

It is more effective in the long term to:
- Focus on success not failure.
- Differentiate objectives, measures and targets for different roles and functions.
- Provide high level, easy to understand measures for high risk areas.
- Provide the ability to demonstrate due diligence in safety management (i.e. being able to verify the effective controls to risks).

Actions
- Change the measures and targets to positive performance indicators.
- Establish measures based on roles and functions.
- Establish a common measurement system for high risk areas.
- Regularly audit compliance with safety systems and accountabilities.
- Analyze incidents and learn from experience.

iv. Complete the planning process.
For each action create measures and targets, define accountability for implementation, cascade the strategy and implement monitoring and reporting processes. Use the monitoring and reporting mechanisms to define future work requirements.

Key Concepts

- Culture is the shared assumptions and beliefs a group of people have about certain behaviors based on what that group values or does not value. The more beliefs people share, the stronger the culture. Culture gives people a framework within which they can begin to organize their world and their behavior.

- To change the culture requires changes to the working organization so that the working environment both enables and sustains the desired culture. This means reviewing and possibly changing:
  - ➢ Managerial leadership practices/behavior.
  - ➢ The organization's systems and structure.
  - ➢ The symbols created in relation to the above, such as recognition, uniforms, car parking spaces and rewards.
- While there is often talk about changing organizational culture, the difficult question is, "What culture do you want to have?" Unless clearly defined, the organization may not achieve the desired change or the newly created culture may not be what was planned.
- The process of implementing a new workplace culture is no different than the process to implement any workplace strategy as outlined in Chapter 3 "Planning, monitoring and reporting for workplace capability".

Tips for Getting Started

1. If you are looking to change your current culture, write a clear definition of the culture you are trying to achieve. Before starting the change process, ensure the whole leadership team agrees with the definition.
2. If you are currently undergoing a cultural change project, assess the changes required to the organizational structure and the systems of work to support the new structure.

Additional information available at www.theleadershipframework.com.au

- Leading change.
- Understanding resistance to change.

- Barriers to continuous improvement.
- Enabling continuous improvement.
- Tools and resources – Leading change checklist.
- Tools and resources – Change management action plan template.
- Tools and resources – Change management communication plan template.
- Tools and resources – Change management systems of work plan template.
- Tools and resources – Change management training plan template.
- Tools and resources – Change management people resourcing plan template.
- Systems of work and culture.
- Setting conditions for constructive working relationships.
- Building trust and a strong manager-employee relationship.
- Working constructively with your own manager.
- Working constructively with specialists and cross functional roles.
- Working constructively with peers.
- Employee accountabilities for safety.
- Manager accountabilities for safety.
- Manager's manager accountabilities for safety.
- Corporate/safety specialist accountabilities for safety.
- Embedding safety requirements in the performance management sequence of work.

Chapter 10

How to improve team capability

Every manager at every level is
accountable to build and lead an
effective team.

WHILE THE FOCUS OF THIS BOOK is on building organizational capability, every manager has a role to play. This is because every manager at every level is accountable to *build and lead an effective team, so that each member is fully committed to and capable of moving in direction set* (The Leadership Framework).

Common strategies to improve team capability

Two initiatives managers can use to improve team capability are to:

- Improve teamwork.
- Individual and team coaching and development.

A. Improving teamwork

Successful managers build a team that works together to deliver business outcomes. For a team to work effectively, it is not enough for a manager to remind team members that 'they are a team' or to 'just work as a team'. For a team to operate effectively, there must be a shared understanding of why the team exists and what it is expected to deliver. This does not happen by accident. Managers must work to create an environment that encourages and supports teamwork. Managers create this environment by:

- Effectively designing roles.
- Aligning the work of their team.
- Clearly assigning tasks.
- Continually setting the context for work.
- Being a role model (of what good 'teamwork' looks like).
- Valuing and recognizing the contribution of each team member.
- Setting expectations for working together.
- Running effective team meetings.

It is the combination of all these aspects of managerial leadership that leads to great teamwork.

i. Effective role design.

The first step in creating great teamwork is effective role design. Well-designed roles, with clear accountabilities, authorities and role relationships, provide clear rules for engagement and enable focused thinking on the work to be done. They enable people to work together productively towards business goals. Well-defined roles, with clear accountabilities and authorities, provide the basic rules of engagement for working relationships. The lack of a good definition of role accountabilities and authorities is a frequent cause of poor performance, organizational conflict and failure to deliver business outcomes. It can cause confusion and uncertainty, overlapping of work boundaries and inappropriate use of authority, ultimately resulting in poor performance and poor morale.

The process for effective role design is:

Step 1: Determine the purpose of the role

When designing a role, it is important to be clear on the work at the heart of the role and how it fits with other roles (i.e. why the role exists). The starting point is to consider:

- The organization's overall strategy and structure, the business unit's function, its limits and relationship to other business units.
- The business unit's objectives.

Roles should never be designed or created to suit the profile or any other requirements of a particular employee. Many organizations spend too much time on building structures for career development and career opportunity or around salary ranges. While this may provide some benefit to individuals from a development perspective, it can result in compromised, confused or overly complicated structures that get in the way of productive working. The structural consequences of what seems to be a reasonable aim of 'creating jobs for good people' include role compression and work being performed at the wrong level or in the wrong part of the organization. Career development can be handled more effectively in other ways.

Step 2: Determine the tasks of the role

To fully understand the requirements of a role, the manager must clearly define the specific tasks of the role. Consider:

- The key accountabilities of the role and how the accountabilities relate to the objectives of the business.

- The key relationships.
- The systems of work that critically relate to the role.

From these determine the task of the role. Next ensure role accountabilities are matched with the required role authorities.

Step 3: Design the role at the right level
A role contains a group of tasks bundled around a level of complexity. A role must be designed at the right level of complexity to operate effectively within the organization's structure. While there will always be work of differing levels of complexity in a role, a role must have a significant portion of the tasks at the level of complexity of the role's most complex task. Otherwise, the role occupant will become bored or frustrated with the work.

Step 4: Define role relationships
Crucial to the design of any role is the clarity of the role relationships. Role relationships, and the authorities that define them, must be specified to enable everyone in the team and organization to work together effectively and collaboratively. Common questions people have are:
- Can I be informed about the work of another and/or receive reports on that work?
- Can I be advised or try to persuade another role – and if so, which role is accountable for the outcome?
- Can I delay something or stop something – and if so, which role is accountable for the outcome?
- Can I require another role to attend a meeting or to monitor the work of another, and if one role does not cooperate, what are the next steps?

Clarity of roles and role relationships set some of the important conditions for team members to work to their full capability and enable all employees to work together productively. An example of defining the working relationship between a specialist planner and a maintenance supervisor is shown in the diagram below.

Defining working relationships

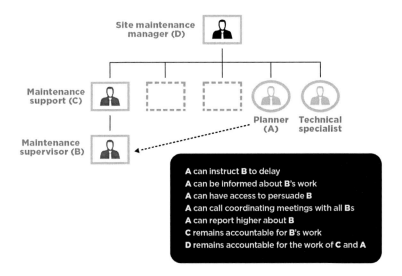

ii. Aligning the work of the team.

Aligning work involves the manager breaking down goals or tasks into parts and assigning accountability for those parts to team members, ensuring all parts of the task are assigned. It also requires each team member to understand how their part of the work fits with other parts. Doing this enables team members to contribute to team outcomes and ensures there is no overlap, duplication or gaps.

iii. Setting clear task assignments.

Managers create the necessary conditions for teamwork by setting clear tasks. People perform their best work when they are:

- Clear about the goal.
- Clear about what is expected and the boundaries within which they must work.
- Given some freedom to determine how they are going to achieve that goal.

To be performed correctly, the tasks must be assigned in a way that ensures team members have a clear understanding of their tasks. For each task, the manager must set:

- The **C**ontext of the task.
- The **P**urpose of the task.
- The **Q**uantity of output required.
- The **Q**uality of output required.
- The **R**esources available to do the work.
- The **T**iming of the above output requirements.

When tasks are clearly defined, team members can use their own judgment to make decisions about their work without constantly referring to their manager for clarification. This enables team members to fully use their capability and improve ways of working.

iv. Continually setting the context for work.

To create a cohesive team, managers must continually set the context for the work of their team. Continual context setting gives team members a broad understanding of what is happening so they can make informed decisions on their work. It ensures they are clear about the degree of freedom and the limits within which to act. It enables team members to collaborate directly and use their own judgment to make decisions about their work. Continual context setting enables team members to fully utilize their individual capability and the capability of other team members to improve the way the work is performed.

Continual context setting is performed by:

- Providing team members with the big picture as it relates to their work.
- Keeping team members informed about the manager's own goals, issues and problems and how successful delivery of the team's work and each individual's own work supports the manager's objectives.
- Providing information on each team member's goals so they can understand each other's assignments and collaborate directly.

A simple process for context setting is:

Provide the background for information > Link to work and events > Explain why the task is required > Provide a clear and concise statement of the purpose of the work/direction

At an individual level, continual context setting is also the starting point from which the manager can address the four key questions that employees need answered to sustain high performance. These are:

- Where are we going?
  (What is our direction? What are our priorities? What do we need to do to be successful?)
- What's my role?
  (What is my part in this?)
- How will my performance be judged?
  (How effective have I been in delivering on my commitments?)
- Where am I going?
  (What is my future in the company? This last question is answered by the manager once removed.)

Continual context setting allows team members to use their individual capability to both complete tasks and to improve the way work is done. It enables high performance.

v. Being a role model.

Managers must demonstrate to their own team what good teamwork looks like. Unless the manager personally demonstrates teamwork on a day-to-day basis, he/she cannot expect it from team members. A manager's own behavior is symbolic, and team members evaluate the authenticity and consistency of the manager's behavior in all interactions. These interactions, on a conscious and subconscious level, form the boundaries within which team members work. Every time a manager fails to demonstrate teamwork, the manager automatically creates new wider boundaries for what teamwork looks like.

vi. Valuing and recognizing the contribution of each team member.

Valuing and recognizing individual contribution is critical to the development of a trusting and productive working relationship. Managers should always be looking for reasons to reward or recognize team members for effective performance. This recognition must be linked to key outcomes such as goals, behaviors or contribution to the team's success.

For recognition to be effective, managers need to understand the work of each team member and their contribution. Recognizing team members for work they have not done, or have not contributed to, can impact the feelings of trust and fairness and discourage other team members (see Chapter 6 "How to retain talent").

vii. Setting expectations for working together.

As work is a social environment where social interaction is required to achieve business outcomes, a clear understanding of the 'social norms' is required. To enable people to work together constructively, managers must set these social norms or expectations. These expectations are fully outlined in Chapter 7 "How to develop workforce capability". The expectations that relate to working together are shown in the table below.

What all employees should do	What employees should not do
• Work together to solve problems. • Accommodate each other's needs as far as possible without changing or compromising their accountabilities or objectives. • Do what is right for the function and the organization even when this may be a potential difficulty for their own area. • Try to persuade their colleagues to take appropriate action that will facilitate the task with which they are involved and increase its effectiveness. • Work together to resolve the issue as they believe their manager would want them to (i.e. within the context of the function and the organization). • Refer to their immediate manager any significant problems that cannot be resolved. Go together to explain what they have done to resolve this themselves and to get clarification on context and what action is appropriate. • When an issue is to be escalated, it should be escalated with full information.	• Cannot tell each other what to do. • Cannot stop each other from taking action. • Should not fight about who is right but focus on the issue. • Never speak negatively about their colleagues. • Do not make judgments about each other's personal effectiveness as they are not accountable for each other's work.

The role of the manager is to ensure team members understand these expectations, to require their application on a day-to-day basis and to hold team members to account for their delivery. Setting expectations empowers team members to do their work. In fact, 'empowerment' is simply another way of expressing that the manager is using all the capabilities of the team, such as encouraging the use of appropriate discretion, encouraging suggestions for improvement and only intervening to set direction and add value.

viii. Running effective team meetings.

To run effective meetings, managers must ensure team members:

- Know the type of meeting they are attending.
- Are aware of the meeting's purpose.
- Understand and fulfill their role and accountabilities in the meeting.

Broadly, managers run two types of team meetings: 'team business meetings' and 'team problem-solving meetings'.

a) Team business meetings.

Team business meetings enable the manager and team members to get together to discuss business issues. They are scheduled regularly, with a fairly standard agenda. Team business meetings provide for regular discussion of the business context, issues affecting the team and the progress towards achieving team outcomes.

The frequency and format should be consistent with the nature of the business and its operations. They should normally be held at least monthly.

The purposes of team business meetings are to:

- Provide and share information.
- Review progress against plans, decide corrective actions, share contextual information.

- Continue the ongoing process of setting context for the team and each individual team member.
- Reinforce values.
- Share ideas and improve the understanding of the business issues affecting others in the team.
- Get a high level of understanding and commitment on actions.
- Assist in implementing change quickly.
- Build trust between the manager and team members and between team members.

Significant problems arising in this meeting are taken 'off line' for dedicated problem-solving.

b) Team problem-solving meetings.

Team problem-solving meetings are established for a specific project or issue and are disbanded when the project/issue is completed/resolved. The purpose of team problem-solving meetings is to use the team's collective mental effort in a goal-directed manner.

Problem-solving meetings are used to:
- Identify or clarify a problem to be worked on and the objectives to be achieved.
- Identify the core issues relating to a problem.
- Analyze issues.
- Generate high-value options.
- Decide actions to achieve the objectives.

B. Individual and team coaching and development

To improve team capability, managers can coach and develop team members in the performance of their current role. There are many ways managers can provide team members with the knowledge, skills and experience required to improve their performance effectiveness. The main methods are:

i. Onboarding new employees (team member induction).

    Induction provides the basic knowledge required to work effectively in a new role. Failure to adequately induct new team members can lead to underperformance, lack of engagement and loss of motivation and may result in the employee choosing to leave the organization shortly after starting. See Chapter 6 "How to retain talent".

ii. On the job coaching.

    Managerial coaching includes:

    - Explaining the full scope and the opportunities of the role.
    - Setting expectations of the need to increase skills and knowledge through improved application (i.e. effectiveness).
    - Providing feedback on the observed work, with advice and/or demonstration on better ways to do things.
    - Developing new knowledge based on the manager's experiences.
    - Resolving problems experienced in the team member's work or working relationships.
    - Bringing behavior in line with organizational values.
    - Addressing any dysfunctional behavior, including a situation where a direct report's personal conduct is adversely affecting others.
    - Identifying specific role-related formal training needs.

    Effective coaching balances the completion requirements of work with the provision of opportunities for people to learn new skills, with guidance and advice. Managers must be careful when coaching to avoid doing the team member's work, even if it takes more time to coach them on a particular task than it would for the manager to do the task.

Coaching does not involve trying to change the individual's values or personality. If behavior is a major inhibitor to performance effectiveness, then the manager must bring this to the person's attention, advise that it is unacceptable and, if necessary, support the employee in getting professional help. If the behavior continues and cannot be changed through coaching in the role, then the manager must initiate removal from the role.

iii. Projects.

Managers can use a wide variety of projects to develop the knowledge, skills and experience of team members. Some examples of projects which may help to develop team members include:

- Planning a conference.
- Installing a new system.
- Integrating systems of work across business units.
- Writing and/or presenting a proposal.
- Writing a press release.
- Launching a new product.
- Managing a change project.
- Doing a competitive analysis.
- Doing a postmortem on a failed project.
- Completing a study on competitors.

iv. Formal training.

Formal training is an important avenue for gaining new knowledge and skills. Often, managers just send team members to training without discussing the manager's expectations. However, training outcomes can be significantly enhanced if the manager plays an active part. To do this, the manager should:

- Carefully assess performance gaps and the training needs that will help to close the gap.
- Review and familiarize him/herself with the training scope, topics and objectives.
- Clearly document the expected training outcomes and agree to these with the team member prior to attendance.
- Reinforce the training outcomes by ensuring their immediate application to the work of the role.
- Make an assessment of the training effectiveness and investment value and report this to the manager once removed (MOR) and human resources.

v. Educational assistance.

Organizations sometimes assist employees who want to complete external study programs to gain required qualifications and skills by providing financial assistance and leave. Managers can discuss such options with team members.

vi. Secondments, rotations and temporary transfers.

Providing work outside of the normal role can be used to:

- Build new knowledge, skills and experience.
- Improve effectiveness in the current role.
- Bring capability back to the business.

These are especially beneficial if they are related to customers (both internal and external), so that the employee can see how the output of their role impacts others, and for improving working relationships.

Key Concepts

- Every manager is accountable to *build and lead an effective team, so that each member is fully committed to and capable of moving in the direction set.*
- Two of the key initiatives to improve team capability are:
  - Improving teamwork.
  - Coaching and team development.
- Successful managers build a team that works together to deliver business outcomes. To do this, they create a work environment that encourages a good flow of information and advice in all directions – top down, bottom up, across the team and the organization. Managers create this environment by:
  - Effectively designing roles.
  - Aligning the work of their team.
  - Clearly assigning tasks.
  - Continually setting the context for work.
  - Being a role model (of what good 'teamwork' looks like).
  - Valuing and recognizing the contribution of each team member.
  - Setting expectations for working together.
  - Running effective team meetings.
- There are many ways managers can provide team members with the knowledge, skills and experience required to improve their performance effectiveness. The main methods are:
  - Onboarding new employees (team member induction).
  - On the job coaching.
  - Projects.
  - Formal training.
  - Educational assistance.
  - Secondments, rotations and temporary transfers.

Tips For Getting Started

1. Create an induction program for a new team member.
2. Allocate a project to a team member designed to improve their knowledge and skills for their current role.
3. Using the 'expectations of all employees' in this book as a guide, explain to your team members how you expect them to work together.
4. Hold a one-on-one meeting with each team member. Discuss the first three of the four key questions that all employees have as they relate to each individual.
5. Before each team meeting, explain the context and the purpose of the meeting.

Additional information available at www.theleadershipframework.com.au

- How managers align work.
- Assessing individual performance effectiveness.
- How to effectively assign a task.
- Managing working relationships.
- Tools and resources – Short guide to managing relationships.
- Managing conflict.
- Quick Guide: Managing performance effectiveness.
- Manager role, accountabilities and authorities.
- Setting conditions for constructive working relationships.
- Building trust and a strong manager-employee relationship.
- Working constructively with your own manager.
- Working constructively with specialists and cross functional roles.

- Working constructively with peers.
- Tools and resources – Sample task assignment example using CPQQRT method.
- Tools and resources – Task formulation checklist.
- Tools and resources – Managerial leadership self-assessment.
- Tools and resources – Manager-team member self-assessment.
- Tools and resources – Manager's team self-assessment.
- Tools and resources – Managerial leadership team feedback.
- Tools and resources – Team member feedback.
- Tools and resources – Sample measures for safety performance.
- Running effective team meetings.
- Team meeting effectiveness assessment tool.
- Meeting Review Checklist.
- Expanded diagram of the teamwork process detailing full accountabilities for the team leader and team member.

Chapter 11

Summary

To improve workforce capability requires more than just training. It requires a planned and integrated approach that also includes the attraction and selection of new employees, retention strategies and the ability to effectively and fairly remove excess employees. It also needs the effective operation of the working organization.

THIS BOOK PROVIDES a model and examples of some of the most common ways organizations can build workforce capability. There are, however, eight general concepts that are key for the development of workforce capability. These are:

1. Having a capable and committed workforce means having:
   - Capable people.
   - An effective working organization.

Both components are necessary.

2. Individual capability is a combination of knowledge, skills and experience, values, preferences and inhibitors and level of work ability. However, each component of individual capability needs to be managed in a different way:

   - Knowledge, skills and experience can be learned through formal training, projects and coaching.
   - Where values and preferences do not align with the current role, then the manager must take action and move the person to a more suitable role. If that cannot be done, then the manager must initiate removal. Training will not assist.
   - Where a person's behavior is inappropriate, the manager must advise the employee. If the employee does not change, then the manager must initiate removal. Training will not assist.
   - If a person's level of work ability is too low or too high for their role, the manager must transfer the person to a more suitable role or initiate removal. Training will not assist.

3. Employee effectiveness is impacted by the working organization, that is, by the organization's structure, design of roles and working relationships, systems of work and managerial leadership practices. These are not training issues. Ensuring the working organization operates effectively will not only improve workforce capability, it will improve individual performance, organizational performance and employee engagement. It will empower people to work to their full potential.

4. The process of creating a good workforce capability strategy begins with an understanding of the business strategy and key workforce issues. In order to create a workforce capability strategy that

supports organizational needs, human resources professionals need to work closely with senior leaders in the organization. Before starting on any workplace capability improvement, have a plan based on research, information and data. The four steps in the business planning process are to:

- Understand the business.
- Identify critical workforce issues.
- Determine strategic options.
- Decide and define initiatives to achieve strategic outcomes.

5. Organizations need an effective strategy imple-mentation process. In some ways, developing the strategy is easy. It is strategy implementation that is the hard part. Strategy implementation has four steps:

- Defining the strategy – Clarifying the strategic objectives and the related initiatives to be implemented.
- Aligning the organization – Getting the organization ready for strategy deployment by aligning the working organization to support strategy implementation, connecting planning and budgeting and allocating accountability and authority at a high level.
- Cascading work – Engaging employees and assigning tasks, with appropriate measures, throughout the organization.
- Monitoring and assuring strategy implementation – Reviewing the progress of strategy implementation and the effectiveness of the strategy itself.

6. Training and development are effective strategies to improve workforce capability but so are attraction, retention and removal of unwanted employees.

- Attracting and selecting capable people is the starting point for an active workforce capability development strategy.
- Retaining capable individuals is essential for organizational success. There is little point in selecting and training capable people only to have them leave after a short period.
- Having the ability to remove people who are excess to requirements or who do not meet the level of performance required, in a respectful manner, is part of a complete workforce capability strategy. So is the ability to manage and engage those who remain.

7. Some interventions, such as cultural change, require the integration of many actions to achieve the required outcome. They require changes to the whole working organization so that the right working environment is created that both enables and sustains the required change. This means reviewing and possibly changing:
   - Managerial leadership practices/behavior.
   - The organization's structure and systems of work.
   - The symbols created in relation to the above.

8. All managers are accountable to *build and lead an effective team, so that each member is fully committed to and capable of moving in the direction set.* Every manager at every level can improve the capability of their team by creating a work environment that encourages a good flow of information in all directions – top down, bottom up, across the team and the organization. Managers create this environment by:
   - Effectively designing roles.
   - Aligning the work of their team.
   - Clearly assigning tasks.
   - Continually setting the context for work.

- Being a role model (of what good 'teamwork' looks like).
- Valuing and recognizing the contribution of each team member.
- Setting expectations for working together.
- Running effective team meetings.

Taking a holistic and integrated approach to workforce capability development will ensure that the organization has the people it needs and operates effectively.

Learn More

Learn more about workforce capability or The Leadership Framework by joining The Leadership Framework Network at www.theleadershipframework.com.au, either as an individual or an organization, and gain access to:

1. Information, tools, templates and checklists that will support you to improve workforce capability.
2. Additional information available on the website includes how to:
   - Improve organizational and individual effectiveness.
   - Improve work systems and processes.
   - Improve managerial leadership at all levels.
   - Create effective organization structures.
   - Create constructive working environments.
   - Implement business strategy.
   - Identify and develop talent.
   - Improve safety performance.
   - Create effective teams.
   - Build teamwork.
   - Build mutual trust and strong manager-employee working relationships.
   - Improve employee engagement.
   - Manage change.

- Manage performance issues.
- Manage strategic relationships.

Alternatively:

1. Read *Leading People: The 10 Things Successful Managers Know and Do* by Peter Mills to gain a better understanding of the role, accountabilities and authorities of managers and learn how to build and lead an effective team.
2. Read *Don't Fix Me, Fix the Workplace: A Guide to Building Constructive Working Relationships* by Peter Mills to identify the main causes of workplace conflict and learn how to create the right working environment to enable and sustain the constructive working relationships that lead to productive work.
3. Read *Make It Work! How to Successfully Implement Your Business Strategy* by Peter Mills to learn about strategy implementation.
4. Arrange seminars/workshops at your workplace on any aspect of The Leadership Framework.

Appendix 1

The Leadership Framework

The Leadership Framework provides managers and organizations with a complete, holistic and coherent system of managerial leadership. It considers the organization as a purpose-built structure, with systems of work and specifically designed working relationships that enable people to work toward a common business purpose. The organization itself is activated by applying effective managerial leadership.

The Leadership Framework describes what all managers must know and must do. It clearly defines the requirements for leadership and sets practical and consistent standards expected of people leaders. Being a holistic framework, it can be used to:

- Improve organizational and individual effectiveness.
- Improve managerial leadership at all levels.
- Improve workforce capability.
- Create effective organization structures.
- Create constructive working environments.
- implement business strategy.
- Identify and develop talent.
- Improve safety performance.
- Create effective teams.

- Build teamwork.
- Build mutual trust and strong manager-employee working relationships.
- Improve employee engagement.
- Manage change.
- Improve work systems and processes.
- Manage performance issues.

The framework's three interconnecting parts provide a set of integrated principles and practices for the organization and for the individual.

Leading yourself is about understanding the role of the manager and how to work with others across the organization, building quality working relationships. It also comprises the essential requirements of what managers need to know about how to deal productively with workplace conflict and people differences.

Leading people is about the things managers must do on a day-to-day basis to manage their team. It comprises the minimum and essential requirements of all people managers from frontline managers up to, and including, the CEO/ managing director. It includes creating effective roles and filling them with good people, assigning and assessing work, rewarding and recognizing good work, building a capable team, enabling continuous improvement, managing change and providing a safe place to work.

Leading the organization is about the additional requirements of managers occupying roles immediately above the frontline manager level. It involves designing the workplace conditions that enable and support productive work, such as organizational structures and systems of work and effective managerial leadership. Business strategy implementation and building workforce capability are part of this.

At the framework's core are strong, two-way, trusting working relationships, focused on achieving business goals.

Using The Leadership Framework enables organizations to operate effectively to deliver strategy. It enables managers to build high-performing teams focused on achieving business objectives. It also enables managers to develop team members to their full potential and to be personally successful.

Origin of The Leadership Framework

At the framework's foundation is a body of knowledge known as Requisite Organization – requisite meaning what is required by the natural order of things. The concepts and principles were originally developed by Dr. Elliott Jaques and Lord Wilfred Brown and are based on significant research and practice around the world. This research considers organizational design as a purpose-built structure, with systems of work and defined working relationships that enable people to work toward a common business purpose. The organization itself is activated by applying effective managerial leadership practices.

The original Leadership Framework was developed by Barry and Sheila Deane from PeopleFit Australasia, who simplified and condensed Jaques' principles and practices.

Using PeopleFit's work, I have complemented, modified and updated it using the research of others and my own extensive experience:

- In senior human resources roles across a range of industries, both in the private and public sector.
- Working directly with my own team as a leader on setting goals and improving performance.
- As an advisor and coach to CEOs, managers and those in non-manager roles in organizations.

The Leadership Framework is the only complete framework for people management.

The Leadership Framework Series

LEADING PEOPLE

- Provides managers with the 10 things successful managers know and do.
- Uses the Leadership Framework to provide you with an integrated approach for how to be successful as a manager.
- Not only does it give you the fundamental foundation for understanding the Leadership Framework, it gives you practical help and tips on how to get started.

DON'T FIX ME, FIX THE WORKPLACE

- Provides an integrated and holistic model for constructive working relationships based on specific understandings of people at work.
- Identifies the main causes of workplace conflict and how to create a working environment that enables constructive working relationships which leads to productive work.
- Defines what organisations and managers must do to create a constructive working environment.

MAKE IT WORK!

- Explains how to successfully implement business strategy.
- Includes key requirements for the organisation's structure (functions, roles and role relationships), its systems of work (policies, processes and information and communication technologies) and effective managerial leadership practices.
- Provides a fully integrated approach to strategy implementation.

THE WAY TO GO

- Provides an effective and usable model for individual and workforce capability development
- Uses integrated approach to workforce capability development which includes the attraction and selection of new employees, development and retention strategies and the ability to effectively and fairly remove excess employees
- Provides specific actions that can be undertaken to improve both individual, team and workforce capability, including talent and critical position management, team development and cultural change.

The Leadership Framework Series is avaiable from

For more information on The Leadership Framework, book reviews, and articles, visit

www.theleadershipframework.com.au